the
new
ceo's
guide

*Advice for the First-Time, Aspiring,
or Current Association Executive*

BETH BROOKS, CAE

★**asae**
association
management
press®

WASHINGTON, DC

The author has worked diligently to ensure that all information in this book is accurate as of the time of publication and consistent with standards of good practice in the general management community. As research and practice advance, however, standards may change. For this reason it is recommended that readers evaluate the applicability of any recommendations in light of particular situations and changing standards.

ASAE: The Center for Association Leadership
1575 I Street, NW
Washington, DC 20005-1103
Phone: (202) 626-2723; (888) 950-2723 outside metropolitan Washington, DC area
Fax: (202) 220-6439
Email: books@asaecenter.org

We connect great ideas and great people to inspire leadership and achievement in the association community.

Keith C. Skillman, CAE, Vice President, Publications, ASAE: The Center for Association
   Leadership
Baron Williams, CAE, Director of Book Publishing, ASAE: The Center for Association Leadership

Cover by Beth Lower, ASAE: The Center for Association Leadership
Text by Troy Scott Parker, Cimarron Design

This book is available at a special discount when ordered in bulk quantities. For information, contact the ASAE Member Service Center at (202) 371-0940. A complete catalog of titles is available on the ASAE website at www.asaecenter.org.

ISBN-13: 978-0-88034-380-0

Printed in the United States of America.

10 9 8 7 6 5 4 3 2 1

CONTENTS

ACKNOWLEDGMENTS

ALTHOUGH MANY PEOPLE THINK OR say, "I should write a book about that," most people do not.

Apparently I often said those exact words out loud, and Becky Faulk, membership coordinator at the Texas Society of Association Executives, finally said, "You keep saying that. When are you going to start writing that book?" Thank you, Becky, for challenging me.

A project like this is a result of cooperation and the experiences of many people. This book is really a compilation of experiences—my 30+ years of experience, the volunteers I have worked with, and the association colleagues that I have grown up with. I give credit to all the volunteer board members and chairmen who taught me how to do a better job, starting with the chairs of the Texas Dental Association. I specifically want to recognize the 10 chairs of the Texas Pest Control Association as well as the 13 chairs of the Texas Society of Association Executives that I have had the privilege of working with.

In addition, the members of the state association community, especially the Alliance of State Associations, have been supportive. In particular, thank you, Jim Anderson, CAE; Wendy Kavanagh, CAE; Leslie Murphy, CAE; Jim Thompson, CAE; Joan Tezak, CAE; and Shane Yates, CAE, for always being my cheerleaders.

Many thanks to Bob Harris, CAE, my mentor and good friend, who never doubted that I could actually write a book. Special recognition to the association executives who contributed examples for the book: Diane James, CAE; Kerry Stackpole, CAE; David Gammel, CAE; Shelley Alcorn, CAE; Greg Fine, CAE; Mary Logan, CAE; George Allen, CAE, as well as Pete Allman, CPA, and Nita Saunders, finance director for TSAE.

To my "kitchen cabinet" who read parts of the book and gave me valuable feedback: JJ Colburn, CAE; Gary LaBranche, CAE; Don Haydon, CAE; Nancy Jones, CAE; Mark Allen, CAE; Robin Painovich, CAE; and Gabriel Eckert, CAE.

Special thanks to Don Haydon, CAE, who was a reader and supporter even before I had an outline and spent hours reading and giving guidance, and to my good friend Mary Lange, CAE, who has always encouraged me and has been interested in hearing all about this writing adventure.

Thanks to the ASAE staff who oversaw the production of this book, Keith Skillman, CAE, and Baron Williams, CAE.

And to the dozens of people who politely inquired, "How is the book going?" You don't know it, but just by asking, you gave me support and encouragement.

This book would never have been done on time without Glen Nelson, writing coach extraordinaire, who cheerfully thought through the content of the book with me and guided me through the book writing process. Thanks to Linda C. Chandler, a fellow Texan with association experience, who edited the final manuscript.

To all the Texas Society of Association Executives members and staff who inspire me, help me, and teach me. What a wonderful community to be a part of!

Special thanks to my husband, David, who took over all the shopping, housework and cooking for four months while I worked on this book. Thank you for encouraging me when I voluntarily took on this "second job" that had such long hours.

And especially to our son, Matthew, who motivates me to do better every day. Please read this book. I think you would make an excellent association professional someday.

FOREWORD
By Bob Harris, CAE

THE CEO JOB DESCRIPTION WAS scribbled on a notepad. The search committee said, "You won't have to do more than get out a quarterly newsletter, report on the finances, and pay the bills."

"Plus, plan our board meetings and annual conference." They wanted to know if you knew QuickBooks and anything about websites. The executive committee said, "We are looking for someone who can just handle all this."

It sounded straightforward. Perhaps even easy.

Well, maybe.

A month later you find yourself doing (or learning to do) strategic planning, selling trade show booths, planning educational programs, reading complex contracts, working on policies, sending out dues notices and following up on collections, speaking to legislators, visiting chapters, and publishing a magazine.

Whew! It seems the search committee conveniently forgot to mention a few things...

There are about 67,000 IRS-recognized trade associations and professional societies in the United States—and perhaps a million associations worldwide. The majority are smaller-staffed associations (fewer than 10 staff). Each association has a board, and often a full-time staff. If you have been hired to be an association executive director (or want to be), what kind of training is needed to lead an association? What are boards looking for? What exactly does an association CEO do?

This book will tell you.

The fact is most association professionals stumble into their jobs. Relatively few have completed a college program specifically in nonprofit management. Many were drawn by the organization's mission, transitioned from serving on an association board, or moved up in an association as a staff member. The majority (in fact, in my experience, the estimate would be more than 90 percent) join the association world by "accident," applying for a vague position that ends as the CEO of an association.

At first the job looks easy: Travel to and attend meetings and let the board make all the decisions. In reality, the job requires that staff and board members work together to manage the equivalent of a fast-paced corporation.

It's not enough to simply serve your stakeholders, or clients, or customers as corporations do. You must also serve your members—the average man or woman who, in general, pays a yearly fee to be a part of your group.

That's where dynamics change.

As an association executive, you must be skilled in volunteer management, governance, project management, office and personnel management, communications, and technology applications. Board leadership also involves sales and marketing, government affairs, and oh...everything else.

Beth Brooks, CAE, the author of this book, has proven herself through 30 years of success. She has a national reputation for innovation and is a respected teacher of association management. The value of this book is the mix of core knowledge and practical experience. Beth doesn't hold back when she shares successes, advice, and best practices. Each chapter provides nuggets and practical advice. One cannot pay enough for the sage counsel that she readily shares. Beth cares about the success of associations, the staff, and the volunteer leaders—by writing this book, she is able to transfer her knowledge throughout the profession.

The New CEO's Guide is a must-read for any newly hired CEO—whether transitioning from a previous CEO position or taking on his or her first CEO job—as well as staff, volunteer leaders, or anyone who aspires to be an association CEO.

If you serve in any capacity as an association leader, the information that follows is simply indispensable.

– Bob Harris, CAE
President, NonProfitCenter.com

CHAPTER ONE

Starting as the Leader of an Association

The first 90 days are critical in learning the association's culture and enlisting the support of the old guard, its legends and leaders. Management processes and staffing may need to be refined, but they can wait. Earn trust by asking, listening and garnering support as the association's new CEO.

– Jimelle Rumberg, PhD, CAE
Executive Director
Ohio Foot and Ankle Medical Association

WHEN I TOOK THE JOB as executive director of a small-staffed statewide association at the age of 34, I thought I knew what I was doing. I came in with training and experience. I was a Certified Association Executive (CAE), and for 10 years, I had served as the communications director for the Texas Dental Association, which had a staff of 12. I had gained self-confidence as I oversaw the meetings (an annual conference of 7,000), communications (monthly magazine), and membership (approximately 8,000 members). I thought I was well qualified to be the executive director of a small association.

I walked into my role as the executive director of the Texas Pest Control Association in Austin, Texas, and quickly discovered just how steep the learning curve can be for new leaders.

The association had no staff and no office. It had previously been run by an association management company, so there was literally no place to work. By necessity, my first task, before my official start date, was to find and lease office space. Even though I wasn't officially on the payroll yet, the next week's tasks consisted of purchasing everything we would need to set up an office—from staplers and paperclips to desks, computers, and phones—and hire an assistant. As I visited with the board chairman that week, I realized that I didn't really understand what pest control technicians do and I needed to know firsthand, so I spent a day riding along with one of his employees to get a feel for their unique responsibilities and challenges.

Somehow, I got all that done in five days. Over the weekend before my first official day on the job, we moved into our new office. If I were tempted to relax and enjoy my burst of productivity, there was no time; during my daily discussions with the association's chairman, I found out that there was a monthly magazine to produce and a conference for 400 attendees just two months away. Neither project had been started.

I hit the ground running. My first official day at the association consisted of a 17-hour road trip to North Texas with the volunteer chairman of the board. We visited several members at their offices, led one conference committee meeting, and attended a Dallas chapter meeting before driving back to Austin. I wasn't overwhelmed at that point, but it was an avalanche of information and responsibility. It actually was a wonderfully informative day for me, and it set the tone for the close collaboration with the chairman throughout his term and the association's success for the next 10 years.

To be honest, if I had known how hard the job was going to be and what I would be expected to handle, I am not sure I would have applied for the job in the first place. Happily, I had youth, exuberance, and desire to do a good job on my side. I was a fast learner (and not afraid of hard work), but in hindsight, I confess that I didn't know very much about running an association. I drew on my CAE training, the good role model of my previous association, and the fact that my new association had wonderfully supportive and smart leaders. These things helped me tremendously during those first years, as I gradually learned how important associations are and how challenging it is to direct one of them.

While I like to think that I was great at learning on the fly, I didn't know anything about association management in the broader context. I knew very little about lobbying, regulatory activities, budgeting, audits, or board governance—that is, how associations function. I knew little of the history of associations in America. These were all areas that I needed to know as the executive director. I wish I had had someone or some book to tell me what I didn't know. It would have saved me a lot of time and frustration.

I came to discover that there are associations large and small in every community in the world. They include associations that represent smaller populations or may be staffed by one employee, niche demographic organizations, such as the Society of Tribologists and Lubrication Engineers, the Dog Behavioral Association, and the Cut Flower Association as well as advocacy powerhouses like the National Rifle Association, the American Dental Association, and the AARP (the American Association of Retired Persons). Whatever the size of the association, each has a specific and necessary function. They are advocates. Their members support and encourage one another as they interact with their communities. They provide communication, education, and networking. They affect how laws are written, how small business owners work locally, and the agenda of national, if not global, politics.

I didn't fully understand that then, and gradually I discovered that associations function differently from other organizations and corporations. Their goals are different. They are structured differently, too, and without understanding that, a new CEO will waste time and become frustrated. As an association executive, you need to understand the foundation, the structure, the politics, and the people within the association. In addition, you need to be constantly scanning the horizon for issues that may affect the members.

The job of the CEO is a combination of 1) working in partnership with volunteer leaders, 2) being visionary, and 3) doing what needs to be done. I should note that the title president, executive vice president, CEO and executive director are interchangeable. My first title was executive director, but some associations, particularly large ones, mirror the vocabulary of the corporate world and use the title CEO.

Fast forward 22 years. I am now the president and CEO of the Texas Society of Association Executives (TSAE), and I find myself counseling dozens of new association CEOs. Many of them are successful people in other endeavors who have just been hired by an association board. Although many have tremendous experience in the business world, as it relates to association management specifically, they are newbies—exactly where I was two decades ago. Most have never worked for an association before, and they have to figure out what an association is; what its culture is like; how it is organized, regulated, and governed; and especially, how it gets things done.

I also speak with new association CEOs who have previously served as association staff members. They want advice about how to make the transition to the top staff position. The third group I find myself counseling is members of a profession who have been hired as their association's CEO (for example, a teacher being hired by an educational association). Perhaps they have served on the board, and certainly they know their industry, but they are new to the concept of running an association. All three groups seek advice: Where do I start, what do I need to know, and what should I do first?

In trying to help them, it became apparent to me that they need a guide: a resource to provide direction for the new CEO about the how-to's of running an association. I searched and found that while there are many books on association management specifics (addressing topics such as association law, working with volunteers, association finances, and so forth), there was no resource to help figure out what to do if you are the new CEO—what questions to ask, what steps to take, what actions to consider, what to be aware of, and who to talk to about your new job. New association executives expressed particular interest in wanting a guide they could read quickly to get an overview and then use as an ongoing reference as needed.

Heading up an association is a unique challenge, and most people who have not had prior experience with CEO responsibilities have little idea what to do or where to turn to for counsel and guidance. Often, they don't want to ask their own board members for advice because they were hired after the association board thought they were qualified and would do a good job. They don't want to appear unprepared. And yet, there is so much to learn or sharpen.

How can you learn it? That is the purpose of this book.

CHAPTER TWO

Understanding the Unique Characteristics of Associations

Focus on what is important versus what is urgent. Often the former is lost in the fog of the latter. Leadership requires CEOs to know the difference.

– Gary A. LaBranche, CAE, FASAE
President & CEO
Association for Corporate Growth

ANY PEOPLE DON'T KNOW WHAT an association is. This is always surprising to me because associations are all around us. Whenever I meet someone new and the conversation gets around to what I do for a living, there is usually an awkward silence when I say, "I am an association executive." They have no clue what I mean. I have learned to explain by turning the question around. I ask them their occupation—teacher, builder, florist, plumber, engineer—and I explain that their profession has an association to represent them. Then the light comes on.

Associations have a rich history in America. Benjamin Franklin founded the American Philosophical Society, the first learned society in the United States, in 1743. (It continues today.) Its early members included Thomas Jefferson, George Washington, John Adams, and Thomas Paine. It attracted the best minds in the country, and its purpose was to explore improvements in American society and to influence policy. It was an organization separate from government and elected office. Over time, the association's members included Darwin, Pasteur, Audubon, Edison, and Lafayette.

Before Colonial America, associations in Europe were formed as early as medieval days so that people with a common interest could influence the government through merchant guilds. Guilds emerged in Europe with the growth of towns in the 10th and 11th centuries. Until this time, merchants had been itinerant peddlers who handled all their own trading transactions, personally traveling from market to market and from town to town. These merchants banded together to protect themselves from bandits as they made their business rounds. Gradually, merchants expanded their activities and delegated tasks like the transportation of goods to others, while the merchants based themselves and their operations in a particular town. The merchants' associations soon became more tightly organized and were legalized and recognized by town governments. These merchant associations, or guilds, became intimately involved in regulating and protecting their members' commerce, both in long-distance trade and in those activities that catered to the needs of the town's inhabitants.

The Power of Associations

Today, associations continue to serve the same general purposes and continue to grow. In 2013, the IRS recognized 66,985 trade and professional associations.

Approximately 1,000 new 501(c)(6) associations are formed each year. For example, the National Association of Bubble Soccer, which represents the full-contact sport whose players wear a plastic bubble five feet in diameter, was formed in 2015. Associations are advocates and educators for professionals in communities large and small. They represent the interests of their members and seek to influence policy on behalf of the interests and needs of their constituents. That's the most basic definition. In practice, however, associations are important entities that are unique in their structure, governance, finances, and goals. Furthermore, I believe it is impossible to understand American business completely without having a firm grasp on the role of associations.

The nonprofit sector as a whole is the second-largest employer in the United States, second only to the government (federal, regional, state, local). It accounted for 10.3 percent of wages and salaries paid in the United States in 2012. (Source: Bureau of Labor Statistics, *The Economics Daily*, Oct. 21, 2014). Membership organizations—including religious, social advocacy, civic and social organizations, and trade and professional associations—employed more than 1.3 million in 2013.

And impressively, the impact of educational meetings alone accounts for $280 billion in direct spending by attendees, with the meetings industry supporting nearly 1.8 million jobs. (Source: *The Power of Associations*, ASAE, January 2015.)

What Kind of Entity Is an Association?

Associations have certain requirements to qualify as legal entities. An association must be primarily (more than 50 percent) devoted to activities in the business interests of members, and it must represent at least one line of business. As a new CEO, it's critical that you understand what kind of association you've been hired to lead and how tax laws affect it. Associations are generally nonprofit in nature, but they are categorized in a specific tax status under the IRS nonprofit umbrella. People assume that since they are nonprofit, associations don't pay taxes. That's incorrect; associations *do* pay taxes. In fact, finances and taxation are unique aspects of associations. It can be a challenge to learn their legal parameters. Which taxes your association pays depends on which IRS tax status your association falls under. For example, a 501(c)(6) pays sales tax on all purchases, while a 501(c)(3) does not. Both pay taxes on payroll.

It won't surprise you to learn that the tax code regarding associations is complex. While there are at least 15 different nonprofit classifications, two cover the vast majority of nonprofits operating in the United States. Those are 501(c)(3) and 501(c)(6). For the purposes of an introduction to the world of associations, this basic knowledge forms a solid foundation.

The 501(c)(6) classification usually applies to business, trade, and professional organizations and chambers of commerce. 501(c)(6) groups are exempt from most federal income taxes. However, 501(c)(6)s are not exempt from federal taxes such as employment taxes, unrelated business income (UBIT), or sales taxes on goods purchased.

Donations to a 501(c)(6) are not tax deductible like a charitable contribution in the 501(c)(3) category. A 501(c)(6) organization may engage in political activities that inform, educate, and promote its given interests.

Professional associations or societies serve individuals who share acquired knowledge or a field of business or practice in a profession, often with a credential. A few examples include the Minnesota Society of Certified Public Accountants, California Dental Association, and American Institute of Architects. Trade association examples include the Florida Pest Control Association, Michigan Heating, Plumbing, and Cooling Contractors, and Texas Nursery and Landscape Association.

A 501(c)(3) must be organized and substantially (80 percent to 95 percent) devoted to one or more exempt public purposes. This tax status is for religious, charitable/philanthropic, scientific, literary, educational, and amateur sports entities. Assets must be dedicated to charitable and educational purposes, and legislative activity must be insubstantial. Donations are deductible as charitable contributions by donors. Examples include the American Diabetes Association, American Cancer Society, and the Oklahoma PTA. A 501(c)(3) does not pay sales tax but does have to pay unrelated business income taxes.

Even for people involved in associations, the notion of profit is confusing. Very often, board members misunderstand the nature of an association's finances. They hear the word "nonprofit" and think that it means "no profit." This is incorrect. An association should be run as a business. In fact, an association will not survive if it does not make a profit. Nonprofits are different from corporations in that all net profits must return to the association, or another nonprofit, unlike a corporation with stockholders, where dividends are paid to the stockholders.

Where Does an Association's Money Come from?

Associations obtain revenues from a variety of sources. For some, dues are a major source. But for many associations nondues income is substantial. Educational meetings, conferences and seminars, exhibits and trade shows, certification and accreditation programs, sponsorships, publication and web advertising, subscriptions, and rental income are all examples of nondues income.

Among the first things you should learn as a new CEO is where your association's money comes from and where the major expenses lie. For many associations, funds are used for program development, including educational meeting costs. According to ASAE's *Associations Matter* (2012), the average trade association spends nearly $1.2 million annually on educational activities, which include publications, conferences, seminars, and other forms of training. The average professional society spends nearly $1.5 million annually on educational activities.

Volunteer organizations and charities may be sustainable by breaking even at the end of the year or dipping into reserves. Often, the question of reserves is debated at board meetings. Should the association take its profit and put it into reserves? Yes!

Why do associations need reserves? The first reason would be for unexpected emergencies. What if a major revenue source like your annual convention and trade show declined drastically because of an economic recession or disaster? Your members may not be able or willing to spend money on travel, hotels, and time away from work, and they may not renew their dues that year. When times get tough, members may cut back, and membership and participation in the association may wane. How would you make up that usually dependable (and budgeted) income?

Another reason to have reserves is for a planned expense that would help the association, including such things as a special membership project, a public relations campaign, a research white paper, surveys, or technology upgrades needed for running the association. And finally, reserves can be used for major planned purchases such as an office move or building an association headquarters. The board decides what the reserves can be used for, and it is important for associations to have them. A rule of thumb for associations is to have six months of operating expenses in a reserve fund. The larger the association budget, the more money should be in reserves.

Why Associations Matter

Very simply, associations enrich our lives. They offer opportunities for volunteerism, and they create standards of safety and quality. Associations keep us competitive by committing resources to lifelong learning, professional development, mentoring, and research. Associations have a positive impact on our future by offering the expertise and perspectives of many to protect, prepare for, and ensure progress in any profession or trade. And associations fuel the economy through industrial development, product and service innovation, and facilitation of domestic and international business.

As an industry, associations shape the regulatory and legislative environment and help determine public policy. Especially on the state and national level, many associations monitor legislation that can enhance or be harmful to the profession or industry, assist in writing bills, and work closely with regulatory agencies. Many associations employ lobbyists to assist them in their efforts. Sometimes smaller-staffed associations have the CEO also serve as a registered lobbyist. In fact, many association CEOs started out working in the legislature or as lobbyists and were later hired as CEOs.

Most associations have a code of ethics, and members must agree to act in the best interests of and fulfill their obligations to the organization and its constituents/members. They are to conduct themselves professionally, comply with all laws and regulations, ensure proper conduct, and act honestly, fairly, ethically.

Some associations increase public awareness through media campaigns about diseases (cancer, diabetes), the environment (recycling), or best business practices (warnings about fake roofers who scam the public after a hailstorm). According to ASAE's *The Power of Associations* (2015), 71 percent of all associations conduct industry research or develop statistics. For example, realtor or homebuilder associations publicize the number of homes sold in the last month or year. The American Dental Association publishes research about oral health or new innovations in dental equipment.

Here's an amazing statistic: Associations are the largest provider of post-college education in the United States. The 2012 "Adult Education Survey" conducted by the National Center for Educational Statistics shows that 57 million adults in America take formal work-related courses or training each year, and more than 69 percent of those individuals receive that training from private businesses or professional associations.

Through continuing education, certificate programs, credentialing, and licensing, associations keep their members up to date, protecting the public and distinguishing members of associations from others in their profession who do not take advantage of this training. Think about familiar designations for certain professions—CPA (Certified Public Accountant) or CFRE (Certified Fund Raising Executive). Such credentials have requirements for achieving and then maintaining the designation. According to ASAE's *Associations Matter*, 36 percent of associations offer credentialing programs that advance a worker's skills, career opportunities, and personal reputation as well as protect the public by ensuring that practitioners meet certain standards of competency.

Most licensed professionals, from doctors and attorneys to plumbers and cosmetologists, are required to obtain continuing education each year to keep their licenses. And this education is offered by associations.

Associations depend on volunteers to help shape their future. What associations do you belong to? PTA, homeowners, sports organizations, fraternities and sororities, alumni, MENSA? Nine out of ten Americans belong to an association. One in four belongs to four or more associations. (Source: Gelatt, J., "Membership Associations," K. Agard, ed., *Leadership in Nonprofit Organizations: A Reference Handbook,* 2011). Associations are vital to the nation, and billions of hours are contributed annually to support their causes. Nearly 63 million Americans contribute nearly 7.7 billion hours volunteering through a membership organization annually; an estimated value of this volunteer service is nearly $173 billion (Source: ASAE, *Power of Associations,* 2015).

Some associations are small and are completely run by volunteers. Others start with part-time staff, and with growth, add additional staff. The largest national association is the American Automobile Association, with 54 million members and 40,000 full-time employees (Source: AAA 2014 Fact Sheet). Some associations are managed by an association management company (AMC). An AMC is a for-profit business whose owner and staff handle the needs of the association (meeting planning, finances, communication, board meetings, and other responsibilities). An AMC can offer "a la carte" options of work to be done and is ideal for an association that does not need to have full-time dedicated staff.

An Overview of Things You Need to Know as CEO

The remainder of this chapter provides a brief overview of association leadership. It might be a review for some executives, but even seasoned professionals sometimes find themselves getting lost in the details of managing an association from time to time and a refresher can be helpful.

You Are Not Alone—Get Connected

Let's say that you are new to the role of an association executive. Most people who start working in an association do not understand that they are a part of a very large profession. In fact, membership organizations employ more than 1.3 million people in the United States. (Source: 2013 Bureau of Labor Statistics' Quarterly Census of Employment and Wages).

Do not fail to tap into resources that will allow you to function more efficiently, to avoid issues that your peers have already faced and solved, and to receive timely information and emotional support. Other association CEOs do what you do. Some are literally down the street or just across state lines. Even though you will be busy in your new position, know that you don't have to operate alone. You will find that most association executives are eager to assist a new CEO. After all, they have all been in your shoes. It's overwhelming to walk into a new position as the association's CEO. Be sure to reach out to others and become connected in the grand network of American associations. These resources will be invaluable to you.

Within the first month on the job, contact executive directors who work for the same profession in another city or state. For example, if you work for the Minnesota Pharmacy Association, you have a peer in many other states. Usually there is an informal (or formal) meeting once or twice a year where all the state/regional executive directors meet to share information and learn about national issues affecting the industry. These colleagues will be helpful to you, as their members are in the same profession or trade as yours, just in a different state.

In addition, if you work for a local or state association, contact the state or national association that represents your industry. These are people you need to know early on. You will see them at industry conferences and legislative visits, and you will share with each other all year long. They are your lifelines, as they are the umbrella association for your industry.

Another suggestion would be to join your local, state, and/or national association of association professionals. These organizations are distinct from your specific organization. They are an association of leaders of a variety of associations (the "association of associations"). Although associations are distinct in their purposes, there is a lot of overlap in the way they are directed. Association executive organizations will offer you the professional education you need to do your job, and they can put you in touch with experienced CEOs located close to you. You will need a core group of colleagues to call when you have questions, need to vent, or want samples or resources. In your state, it may be called the (state) Society of Association Executives. On a national level, the American Society of Association Executives also offers education and other resources. Both offer conventions, seminars, online education, online resources, and professional staff to assist you and your staff as well as resources such as referrals to vendors, attorneys, and financial advisors. In addition they have samples and templates for many association-related needs, such as a request for proposal (RFP) for a meeting or for an audit, CEO contract, record retention policy, personnel handbook, and policies on conflict of interest, antitrust, and more.

Many leaders of associations are unaware of these valuable resources until a couple of years into the job. And they regret not knowing about them or taking advantage of all the education they could have received (and avoided a lot of needless aggravation). Furthermore, these resources could have provided much-needed help and shortened the learning curve.

Association Documents That the Leader Needs to Understand

Governance is broadly defined as the way things get done through the organization's structure. Governance includes the decision-making units of an organization, their powers, authorities, and responsibilities. Governance is about oversight, processes, and accountability. Typically the organization's bylaws describe the governance structure, relations with affiliated groups or components, and how power is allocated within the association.

If you have not worked for an association before, you should be aware of key guiding documents. First, every association has a mission. Seek to understand the particular mission of your association and ensure that organizational documents regarding it are current and clearly stated. This will serve as your roadmap in decision making, strategy, and governance.

Everything the association does should relate to its mission statement; it is what the association stands for. The mission statement should be easy to remember, short, and to the point. Mission statements express how the association will make a difference as a result of what it is doing.

If the association can clearly define and adhere to its mission, then it will avoid the distractions—however well-intentioned—that can potentially derail it. Every project or undertaking by the association should mesh with the mission statement. It is tempting to ignore the mission statement when some worthy cause or new idea comes along. Because associations are service oriented, their members want to help, especially in times of a crisis. For example, after 9/11, many associations coordinated volunteers to assist, and in that case, it was usually part of their mission. The Texas Counseling Association sent counselors to help victims' families; the National Association of CPAs sent members to help survivors by offering free advice and services. The National Association of School Psychologists (NASP) developed materials about grief, trauma, and other topics related to crisis recovery. Those materials were translated into six languages; collaborative relationships were established with educational associations; and NASP continues to provide resources to its members for traumatic events such as SARS, tsunamis, and hurricanes.

But sometimes members suggest activities that fall outside the mission of the association. Such initiatives can drain the association's resources and personnel and make the association lose its focus. The mission statement serves as the go-to guide when association leaders start to veer off course or when a member has an idea that is not aligned with the mission of the organization.

One accounting association had a member who suggested the association help a country devastated by an earthquake. The suggestion was to buy, ship, and distribute recycled computers to the country, providing a public service. Yes, that is a great idea and a worthy sentiment. But the cost and manpower that was needed did not align with the association's mission, which was to support accountants. Another member, referring to the mission, suggested an alternative: sending a donation instead of setting up a full-blown program that required management and on-going support. Great solution. And members felt satisfaction in being able to offer this support.

Other framework documents you need to understand are the organizational documents legally required of every association. They include the Articles of Incorporation, which is an agreement between the association and the state defining the organization's legal purpose and its tax-exempt status. It establishes the legal basis for the organization's existence, and you must have this to apply for nonprofit tax-exempt status.

Next come bylaws. Bylaws are an agreement between the association and its members, defining who can participate in the association and how they do so. Some of the most important provisions for bylaws include indemnification (a statement that limits the personal liability of the board members), member eligibility and rights, board and officers' criteria (including titles and descriptions, minimum and maximum number of board members, number required for a quorum, board terms, procedure for removing a board member, number of board meetings per year, and voting by electronic means), the nomination process, and standing committees.

When making decisions, always refer to the bylaws. When the bylaws do not address a situation, you can refer to your state's nonprofit law and/or your attorney. Bylaws are broad by nature, because changing the bylaws usually is not easy and often requires a membership vote. (The process for how to amend the bylaws should be in the bylaws.) For example, bylaws should not spell out how much the dues are, specific dates when the annual conference will be held, or dates of board meetings. Thoughtful consideration should be made when amending bylaws. If changes are made, the revised version should be kept in your master file, and copies of the updated bylaws given to the board members, put on your website, and well publicized. Bylaws lay out the "rules of the road" for association governance, and periodic review of the bylaws should become part of the association's ongoing governance review.

Policies and procedures round out the organizational documents. Policies set specific mandates for action and decision making. A board policy manual is important because it includes all the policies approved by the board as well as governance policies. Minutes of board meetings should be kept in a secure location for historical and legal reasons. And finally, the association's operational procedures, which are step-by-step processes detailing how to accomplish tasks in the organization, are important documents.

Understanding the Finances of an Association

Mastering the intricacies of association financial practices will be crucial to your ability to lead, particularly as boards of directors come and go. You will find yourself as a gatekeeper regarding financial knowledge. It is not a responsibility that you can ignore or delegate. You simply must know about your budget and where the association stands financially.

If your background is in the for-profit world, you will find the finances of an association different. There won't be earnings to look at each quarter and to try to beat, for example. Profits are not released to shareholders, rather, are used by the association to further its goals as it sees fit. In addition, unlike the corporate world, association board members are generally not paid for any work they do; they are volunteers. They can be reimbursed for travel or approved out-of-pocket expenses, and there should be a policy explaining who can be reimbursed and for what purposes. I recently heard about a member coming to the association office when a committee meeting was being held. He was not a member of the committee, but he asked to sit in and listen. The staff didn't think anything of that situation until they received an expense report from the member requesting reimbursement for his flight, hotel, and food for attending the committee meeting. Fortunately, this association had written policies in place to reimburse volunteer committee members only, and that policy helped them explain to the member why his expenses would not be reimbursed. In the big scheme of things, the amount of money was not a concern. What could have been a concern was if the association did not have a policy. Then it would have had to negotiate with a member without any supporting reasons.

As the CEO, you need to understand financial terminology and know how to read financial reports. Does the association operate on an accrual or cash basis, for example? If you don't know and you don't have a staff bookkeeper or accountant, find out if the association has an auditor or contract accountant that you can learn from. You need to understand the financials and raise concerns if budgeted revenues are not being met or if expenses are out of line. Boards will forgive many things but not consistently bad financial performance. Know your budget. Know the numbers. Any decisions about expenditures that are not in the approved budget should be approved by a motion from the board. If a program/service does not work out financially, you should be the first to identify the issue and communicate quickly with the board. Be clear about the explanations and what the next steps will be to address problems. Don't sugarcoat the bad news. Failure is simply a consequence of risk. It happens in every organization. Covering up financial problems, however, is a completely separate issue, and it is unacceptable.

It is important for the board of an association to get regular financial reports and that the financial condition of the association be reviewed at all board meetings. Most associations have an executive committee member who serves as the board treasurer or chairman of the finance committee. Sometimes a finance committee regularly reviews the finances. As the leader you will want to ensure that you are doing everything you can to be transparent about the finances as well as the processes you have in place to oversee the financial administration of the association. Nonprofits are teeming with potential fraud and other abuses of finances. For now, it is sufficient to say this: Stay on top of financial oversight and reporting.

Having a finance committee does not release the board of its duty to oversee the financial health of the organization. It is also important for board members to understand how to read and interpret the financials. Sometimes board members who are well versed in finances may not understand nonprofit accounting and how to read the financial reports. Therefore, going over the financial report carefully with all new board members is important. Be sure to explain the large revenue areas as well as variations from budget to actual expenses. You may find the best time for training is during board orientation. Some associations bring in their staff accountant or CPA from their accounting firm to explain the budget and finances and to assist with orienting the board and helping them understand budget to actual, balance sheets, and other accounting jargon.

As a new CEO, don't withhold financial bad news from the board. Sometimes new CEOs arrive to find that the financial health of the association is in trouble. Financials may have been misstated, reserves may have been spent, and the board may have been misled or kept in the dark. I know of associations where the new CEOs had to tell their boards that the organizations had little to no money. Drastic cuts had to be made and staff let go. Do not be timid about advising the board if you uncover mistakes or misinformation. The board must know the situation and work on a solution with the CEO.

Each association should have an annual budget. As the new CEO, you will want to review the budget as soon as possible. This will give you a real sense of the main revenue and expense items and how they compare to the prior year. Is the revenue diversified or is the majority from one or two events or dues? If the bulk of your revenue is from one or two sources, that may be a future concern. If something happens to those sources, the association could suffer. If there are drastic actual to budget variations during the year, you need to keep the board apprised of the situation.

Note, if you have subsidiaries, such as a foundation or a political action committee, they will have separate budgets.

Many associations have an annual audit conducted by an accounting firm. While not legally required to maintain nonprofit status, having an annual financial audit is a best practice. Several firms specialize in audits for nonprofits. Just knowing that it has an annual audit will tell you a lot about the association. If there's no audit, ask why. If the association has had an audit, read the auditor's management letter to learn about any concerns the auditor has, such as fraud or lack of segregation of duties. If there are concerns, ask what has been done to remedy those concerns. An audit report is to be reviewed and approved by the board, and noted in the board minutes.

An important filing that you need to know about is the IRS Form 990, which is a public record. The Form 990 is an annual reporting return that certain federally tax-exempt organizations must file with the IRS. If a Form 990 is an unknown entity to you, ask a CPA to help you understand the importance of the filing. The board should review and approve the annual Form 990, so check the past minutes to make sure that has been done. The 990 asks questions about the filing organization's mission, programs, policies, and finances, including staff compensation information, so while you are studying the form, look at how the association answered the policy questions and ensure that those policies be developed if any have the answer "no."

Every new CEO should contact the association accountant, auditor, and retirement advisor as soon as possible. If the association has reserves that are invested, talk to the investment advisor as well. These professionals will be a great resource to you in understanding the financial condition of the association.

Working with the Board of Directors

Associations are led by a volunteer board of directors. The board of directors is the main governing/decision-making body (although some associations have a House of Delegates as well). The CEO is an advisor, not the final decider or controller. The CEO is a partner of the board leadership and is responsible for ensuring that the board members have all the necessary and available information to make informed decisions. The board function is threefold: direction setting, policy making, and evaluation/accountability. Direction setting includes strategic planning and vision for the association; policy-making is evaluating and approving the policies, including governance policies, legislative policies, member policies, or standards of practice policies; evaluation/accountability refers to evaluating the programs and services offered by the association, the board itself, and the CEO.

Strategic Planning

Planning is another one of the principal duties of an association board. Most associations go through a strategic planning process every year or every other year, usually involving the entire board and sometimes committee chairs or other key members. It can be done in a retreat setting, with one or two days spent on creating several large initiatives to move the association forward. Depending on the needs of the association, it can also be done in one day or even just a few hours. The time and location considerations all depend on what you need at the time.

The strategic plan serves as the roadmap for the association and staff. Think of it as an action plan for your mission statement. If it is vague and unfocused, you are likely doomed to ineffective work. A bad strategic plan is a recipe for frustration. A solid plan drives your efforts forward and focuses the association on common goals. Having a strategic plan as the guiding document for a couple of years ensures that the entire board supports the plan and agrees on its priorities. It shows the staff what to work on. Years ago, associations commonly developed 10-year plans, but given the dynamic pace of change and technology today, strategic plans are usually being developed for no more than three years.

If you are new to the association, you'll want to locate the most recent strategic plan. Not having some type of agreed-upon plan increases the likelihood that resources will be used (and misused) in a willy-nilly fashion, based on the principle that the squeaky wheel gets the grease. I have observed that a lax attitude toward strategic planning has the unintended consequence of allowing the chairman to push through pet projects, whether or not it is in the best long-term interest of the association. While being chairman deserves respect, allowing a chairman to change the direction of the association each year is a recipe for disaster. The chairmanship changes annually. Are you willing to change the direction of the association every year? It should not be up to the chief elected volunteer to decide what the priorities are going to be. Having a strategic plan is essential for a board to do its work. Together, board members agree on what is important, and they direct the association staff to execute it. The strategic plan is a board decision, and those discussions should be held during a well-planned, fact-based strategic planning session.

Working with Members and Volunteers
Associations are membership organizations, and the needs of members will be a paramount concern for you as you lead the association. Volunteers are another important component of associations that are different from the business landscape. Learn how to best use volunteers and put their talents to work.

Members of associations pay dues to receive services and benefits. These benefits vary but usually include reduced prices on continuing education (conferences, tradeshows, seminars, and online education), legislative and regulatory representation, industry information, career growth opportunities, research, philanthropy, access to professional colleagues, and other resources.

Networking (36.6 percent), access to technical information (46.2 percent), and professional development (46.2 percent) are among the most important association functions that motivate members to join associations. (Dalton and Dignam, *The Decision to Join*, ASAE, 2007).

In the study "Membership Matters" conducted by John Wiley & Sons in March 2015, academic professionals reported that the most appealing elements of society membership are access to peer-reviewed journals (27 percent), continuing education and training (26 percent), and publications about trends and techniques (9 percent). Many respondents indicated they joined an academic association because of the quality of research content, prestige of the organization, and networking opportunities. The most common way that members reported engaging is by reading the publications, followed by participation at annual meetings, and attending area events.

Most associations have industry members and supplier/vendor members as well as other categories of membership (student, honorary). All classifications should be spelled out in the bylaws. While suppliers/vendors/affiliates join the association for different reasons, it is important to understand the value that these members bring to the association and how they are treated within the association. Suppliers want access to the association members, and many want visibility to market their products and services. Suppliers support the organization through sponsorships, exhibiting at tradeshows, and education about the latest products and services.

Depending on the organization you work for, you may see your association members frequently, just during the annual convention, or as you visit their areas. It is important to get out and meet members to learn what concerns they have, see how they work, and really form meaningful relationships. You are not an elected official, but think of members as the people you represent. Be their advocate. You can't know what they need unless you meet them and know them.

Working with volunteers is a big part of being an association leader. Volunteers make up the committees that plan and research so many projects and interests of the association. Many smaller-staffed associations rely heavily on their members to do a large part of the actual hands-on work. A small-staffed association just can't do all the work that is needed, and it is vital to have volunteer assistance. For planning a convention, for example, many associations appoint members to handle speaker selection, onsite registration, evening social events, and other details. To assist these volunteers, the association does a lot of training and produces detailed outlines for volunteers to follow. There can be months of planning leading up to an event and then onsite work to be done. Remember that there should be accountability, especially if there are expenses and financial oversight.

At the pest control association where I worked, a large auction was held each year to raise money for the political action committee (PAC). Volunteers handled getting all the auction items, hiring the auctioneer, planning the schedule, and executing the event. Staff was on site to collect payments and ensure that monies were accounted for accurately. Volunteer members worked hard for months and secured incredible items. Their networks of friends and business partners were so much greater than what the staff could have imagined, and their passion was unexcelled. The result was a successful event each year and a lot of money raised for the PAC.

There is not a right or wrong way to use volunteers; each association has a culture that has developed over time by necessity, by trial and error, or for political reasons. Understanding what work needs to be done by volunteers and what is best done by professional staff is part of the culture, part of what you will be assessing in your new role.

Adapting to the Culture

The culture of an association is as individual as a fingerprint. Very often, the failure of an association executive is connected to his/her inability to understand the culture and nurture it. So what exactly is the culture of an association? It is difficult to quantify because it involves many intangible things, including how the members view themselves, how they treat each other, how events are run, how the staff collaborates, how welcoming the industry or profession is to new members, and how the association holds its meetings. Regarding office culture, associations are distinct from corporations and other organizations. It's entirely possible, for example, that a big manufacturer has employees who don't particularly care about their products and services; it's just a job. In my experience, such indifference rarely occurs in an association. It's actually remarkable. If you choose to work for an association for high school football coaches, for example, or human rights agencies, or professionals in the fields of the arts, sciences, or medicine, you care about that field. Your job takes on the importance of a calling. There is almost a zealous atmosphere surrounding the work. Associations regularly attract people who care deeply about the cause the association represents, even if it is simply to further the abilities of those professionals to do their jobs better. They tend to be loyal to the association, and they stay in place for years, even decades. This, too, is different from corporate America today, and it brings its own set of challenges.

During your interview for the CEO position, you should have sensed (or perhaps had explained to you) the culture of the association and its board. Are the members successful self-employed entrepreneurs with family members in the business? Is there a lot of competition among members, leading to some posturing and possible mistrust? Is there a relaxed atmosphere? Is the board hierarchical, allowing little interaction with regular members? Do members enjoy socializing with each other and forming long-standing personal relationships? Are the board members experienced volunteers? Do they trust and support the staff and CEO? Are their passions and political views on display? Is the association innovative, or is it very traditional with strong feelings about keeping things the same? Is the board developing strategies to move younger members into leadership roles?

How much do the board members value professional staff, their own continuing education, willingness to take risks, and following policies? Is the board transparent in communications with the members? Is it strategic in board discussions or does it micromanage instead? The board culture should be one of strategy, attention to finances and resources, and transparency. Do the leaders have integrity? Are they aligned with the national association—if so, what is that culture? How quickly you "get" the culture, make adaptations to your work style, and establish trust is a critical factor to your success. You can't swim against the tide. Many of the executives who leave associations after brief tenures simply couldn't adapt to different cultures.

Fostering Servant Leadership

Servant leadership is the term that describes how staff members treat association members and the philosophy of putting others first. The staff exists to further the mission, assist the members and to recognize their efforts as volunteers. Staff members are paid to work for the association—members give freely of their time, expertise, and money to support the association. The association belongs to the members. Without members, there would not be an association, and staff would not have jobs. This should be the mantra of every association executive: Members come first; it is their association, not ours. In my experience, most successful leaders of associations do not have big egos; they focus on the members, not themselves. Having the ability to lead and perform and allow credit to volunteer leaders and staff is important.

A new CEO told me how he had worked hard on his association's annual meeting, and it had gone well. However, he was upset because at the general sessions of the convention, the volunteer leaders were recognizing and thanking each other for the successful meeting, and thanked him publicly only once! He was angry that they did not recognize him more, and credit him for the success of the meeting. Creating an environment in which volunteers are given the recognition is one factor in creating a successful association. While we all like recognition, if you have an ego that needs constant stroking, being an association chief executive is not the job for you.

When it comes to leadership, the relationship between you and the chief volunteer leader is critically important. Conflict, withholding information, posturing, power struggles, or manipulation will be obvious to all the board and staff. You want to have an open, collaborative partnership and be a great model for the rest of the organization.

Ensuring Accountability

Finally, as a new CEO, you should be aware of your accountability and how, as a leader of an association, you hold a trust that must not be betrayed. While the board of directors is the governing body, the CEO must help to ensure that several areas are always monitored and held first and foremost in the minds of members and staff. These include operational efficiency (finances, staff), direction setting (mission, governance, strategic plan), and oversight of the association. The CEO provides continuity from year to year and ensures focus on getting to where the board agreed to go. The chief elected volunteer leader comes and goes each year or two. The staff, on the other hand, led by the CEO, gives the stability that ensures direction and operational consistency. The CEO must ensure that financial information is accurate and is available to the members or donors and, in some cases, the public. The CEO must ensure that activities, financials, and reports are monitored and filed on time and that systems/processes are in place to minimize fraud or theft. Staff must be held accountable for their work via regular evaluations. By working as a partner with the board, the executive director's job is to carry out the strategic initiatives created by the board.

Obviously, there are many facets to association management, and each association has unique characteristics and challenges for its staff leader. The following chapters will delve into the issues that you will face as a new CEO.

CHAPTER THREE

Orienting Your Board to Its Work

Assess the board's priorities and commit to those actions first. Sounds obvious, but too often that is not done. Ensure you have good policy and processes in place on how the board operates and make sure you are all on the same page from the beginning.

    – Tom Chapman, CAE
    Executive Director
    American Orthodontic Society

P RESIDENT THEODORE ROOSEVELT LED THE nation through a time of turbulence. In the early 20th century, the United States was becoming a global industrial power, and it faced many growing pains. Roosevelt's slogan, "Speak softly and carry a big stick," is probably his most famous quotation, but in truth, he was a peace-time president, a winner of the Nobel Peace Prize, and a builder of stronger communities that aimed to improve the lives of all citizens. In 1908, he said, "Every man owes part of his time to the business or industry to which he is engaged. No man has a moral right to withhold his support from an organization that is striving to improve conditions within his sphere."

This quotation from President Roosevelt is one of my favorites. It epitomizes the essence of associations. He understood the power inherent in associations, and he encouraged everyone to participate. One of the legacies of Roosevelt— as well as the founding fathers who were members of local associations—is a desire for mutual improvement, accomplished by ordinary citizens deciding to make a difference in their professions and communities.

A common way for citizens to give back to their industry is through service as an association member. Many people find this work highly satisfying. Serving on a board of a professional association is usually a high point of a member's career, and to be chairman brings even greater respect and honor. However, while members are accomplished in their own business endeavors, that doesn't mean they know what they're doing as board members. The unique structure of associations practically guarantees that anyone joining a board of directors needs training to understand the role, be effective, and help the association thrive.

In assisting association executives, I often hear about problems dealing with board situations, even in mature associations. Most often the situations could have been mitigated through clear policies and training board members about their roles and responsibilities. As the new CEO, you want to review the board policies and find out what kind of training has been given in the past. In many cases, I have found that association executives have ignored or been unaware of orientation training for board members. If board members don't understand the structure of the organization, the association's policies, and strategic initiatives, they tend to create and lobby for their own pet projects. That is one consequence of inadequate training, but there are many others. Inadequate orientation for board members can be a red flag for the new CEO, and you will need to have a candid conversation with the chairman to understand why board training has not been held.

For many new CEOs of small to mid-sized associations, an unproductive or dysfunctional board situation can be disconcerting to discover. You may find that board meetings are not organized; board members are missing meetings; no one wants to serve on the board; the board does not want to use savings (ever); agendas are unproductive; and the chairman, while well intentioned, does not really understand what to do or even how to run a meeting.

Sadly, I've seen where this leads, and it isn't pretty. Board members may defer to established, successful board members—whatever they say, everyone agrees with, often shutting down valuable discussion. Perhaps board meetings become contentious, with arguments and heated discussions that go nowhere. Or the meetings become so boring and unproductive that members become completely disinterested and unengaged. It is like a house of cards teetering on the verge of collapse—all because the chairman and the board members lack the appropriate skills to make things run smoothly and accomplish the organization's goals.

It's straight-forward, really, to guide a productive and informed board. It is your job to help them understand the role of a board. Elected board members are bound by three legal duties: duty of care; duty of loyalty; and duty of obedience.

Duty of care means that the officers and directors should exercise ordinary and reasonable care in the performance of their duties, exhibiting honesty and good faith. They must act in a manner that they believe to be in the best interest of the association. The "business judgment rule" protects officers and directors from personal liability for actions made in poor judgment as long as there is a reasonable basis to indicate that the action was undertaken with due care and in good faith. As a board, members need to be aware that whatever actions they take, if not in good faith or in the best interest of the association, could lead to a lawsuit.

Duty of loyalty concerns faithfulness. Chairman and board members must give undivided allegiance to the association when making decisions affecting the association. They cannot put personal interests (outside business, financial interest, family member interests) above the interest of the association. Board members must disclose *all* potential conflicts of interest, and they should recuse themselves from deliberation and voting on matters in which they have personal interests. If board members are also on competitors' boards, they need to disclose that fact and not vote. Strangely, conflict of interest is a subject that some boards never discuss. That's unfortunate because such lapses in judgment could result in a legal infraction or, at the very least, embarrass, alienate, or anger members. Each association should have a conflict of interest policy that the board members sign each year. It is inevitable: There will be conflicts of interest. The solution is to be open about them, identify them, and discuss them. Then the board will decide if the situation is truly a conflict or not. Having a conflict of interest is not the problem; failing to react to it appropriately is the problem. As the new CEO, you might create scenarios where there could be a conflict of interest and then have the board discuss them at a board meeting to understand how the identification and resolution might play out. This might help board members understand exactly what some conflicts could be.

Duty of obedience requires officers and directors to act in accordance with the organization's articles of incorporation, bylaws, and other governing documents as well as applicable laws and regulations. Association policies cannot be ignored. Board members who do not abide by the bylaws and willingly ignore them can get the association into a lot of trouble. The CEO also needs to understand the bylaws, and if the board is discussing an issue that could be in violation of the bylaws, the CEO needs to step in and remind the members of the bylaws. For example, one association's board wanted to bypass the election process and just renew some current board members whose terms were up. They could not find anyone to run for the board and thought it would be easier and faster to just renew board terms without notifying the members of the slate and having them vote, which was the process the bylaws outlined. A board cannot ignore the bylaws.

Perhaps guiding an association sounds a bit daunting, and it should; it's serious business. Some board members have no idea when they take an oath or agree to run for the board that their future actions could have legal ramifications. Association CEOs must understand these duties and explain them to the board. If you find that they have not had training, set up a board orientation session for the entire board. Once they have been educated about their roles and responsibilities, they must keep these matters in mind as they get to work.

Roles of the Board

It is very important for the board to understand its duties and role. Board members have been elected and should take pride in serving in the highest positions of the association. It is your job to help them succeed and to get them the training they need.

The board's roles include:

1. Determine the mission and purpose.
2. Recruit and orient new board members; assess board performance.
3. Ensure effective strategic planning.
4. Select the chief executive.
5. Support the CEO and assess his/her performance.
6. Ensure adequate financial resources.
7. Oversee the resources (budget and financial controls).
8. Determine, monitor, and strengthen programs and services.
9. Enhance the organization's public image.
10. Ensure legal and ethical integrity and maintain accountability.

Orienting Board Members about Their Role

Ensuring that the board members understand their roles is important in the overall success of an association. As a new CEO, you must determine if they have had orientations before. If not, plan on creating a board orientation session as soon as possible. The primary purpose of board orientation is the transmission of information to improve understanding and governance. Board orientation is one of the most important jobs you have as an executive director.

Although they come to association service with years of experience in their fields, many board members have never served on a professional board. They may have been on a committee or perhaps have been involved in boards of Little League, local PTA, homeowners associations, and so forth. Many association CEOs have served in those types of organizations as well. Think back to your own experience: What kind of training did you get? If you were lucky, some type of organized training was provided, but more often than not, there is none. When I was asked to serve on various volunteer-run organization boards, there was no introduction to the organization, no training about my role, no history of actions, and no updates about what they were working on. It was trial by fire. I just had to sit there and listen and try to grasp what was going on. I could either be reconciled to the idea of doing nothing for months until I got the gist of what they were doing, or I could ask lots of questions before, during, and after the meetings. I chose the latter. As the paid staff professional, you don't want your board members—who set the annual goals and do your evaluation—to be in a similar, frustrating situation. So it is important for you to take a good look at your organization and understand how informed the board members are on their roles and then make a plan for how you can best give them the tools and information they need.

Preparing an organized, thoughtful training program for the board is a crucial part of your job. I have had long-time executive directors tell me that they orient the new board members by pulling them aside right before the first board meeting and telling them to just listen, and they'll catch on in no time. That is not board orientation.

You need to know what has been done in the past by the association. Has there been any board orientation? If so, how frequently? Review what was covered in the past. Think about who should attend and who should present the session. Does the whole board attend or just the new members? How long should the orientation last? Is it a focused, stand-alone program or is it tacked onto the beginning of the first board meeting of the year? After reading this chapter, you should have a good grasp on what a good orientation program looks like so you can either tweak your existing program or start a new annual training event for board members.

Whether you are changing an existing program or suggesting the development of an orientation session from scratch, talk with the chairman first. Explain that the best associations have this process in place and you can reference ASAE's study in which seventy-nine percent of respondents indicated having a formal orientation program for their board members (Source: ASAE, *Benchmarking in Association Management: Governance Policies and Procedures,* 2011). The most common excuse why associations don't have orientations is the perception that they take too much time. My experience proves the opposite. An orientation can be conducted in as little as 60 minutes, but typically it is two hours. That is a small investment to promote improved understanding and governance.

Before talking to the chairman about instituting or improving an orientation, you'll want to create an agenda for what would be covered in an orientation session. The chair may want to form a task force to review this proposal, or he or she may unilaterally agree that orientation is needed and then inform the board.

Holding an orientation for the full board or new board members allows you the time to fully explain their roles and responsibilities, any legal concerns, and the organization's finances and strategic initiatives. You may decide to bring in an outside association consultant to facilitate the orientation. Often, hearing this information from an association expert is more powerful than hearing it from staff, especially when talking about roles and responsibilities of the CEO versus the board. Even if you bring in a consultant, there are some association-specific topics that you should cover as the CEO, including the strategic plan, financials, and policies. This is your opportunity to show your knowledge of the internal operations, introduce the staff, explain any issues of concern that you have uncovered, and update the board about trends in the industry that may affect the association.

Bob Harris, CAE, founder of The Nonprofit Center and association consultant, lists the following excellent reasons why you should do board orientation. I recommend that you use these points as part of your discussion with the chairman if you have never had an orientation and as your outline for orientation training if you are doing it on your own.

- **Legal Protection for the Board.** The board should be aware that directors and officers (D&O) liability insurance defends against a suit. Protection is supplemented by the doctrine of volunteer immunity, indemnification, and the corporate structure. If you don't have D&O insurance, you will want to talk with your chairman and recommend that the association purchase this insurance. Telling the board what insurance coverages the association has should be part of the orientation.

- **Documentation.** Directors must comply with the fiduciary principle of "duty of obedience." It requires that they abide by the governing documents (articles, bylaws, and policies). If a court were to ask a director, "Did you receive the governing documents?" the minutes should affirm that they were officially distributed or accessible at orientation. Review the bylaws and board policies during orientation and have board members sign a commitment form acknowledging they understand their roles. A commitment form, that each board member signs and is kept in the office, confirms that the member understands and will abide by association policies such as conflict of interest and antitrust. If an issue comes up during their term, you can refer to the commitment form that they signed.

- **IRS Form 990.** On this required form, the IRS asks a series of questions, including whether the board reviewed the IRS Form 990 prior to its submission. Orientation is an opportunity to acquaint directors with the latest return. After that, the Form 990 should be reviewed and approved during a board meeting each year.

- **Public Records.** Volunteers may think the organization's minutes, finances, and rosters are subject to open record laws and the Freedom of Information Act and that they must give these to any member who requests them. This is not entirely accurate. Inform the board that the IRS Form 990, the Application for Exemption: Form 1023 or 1024, and the Letter of

Determination are public records, and educate the board regarding the potential fine for not making these three IRS documents available upon request. Failure to provide the documents may subject the association to a penalty of $20 per day for as long as the failure continues, up to $10,000.

Copies must be provided immediately (or by the close of business on that day) in the case of in-person requests and within 30 days in the case of written requests. Reasonable copying fees and postage may be charged.

Associations should have procedures so staff members know of the public record IRS requirements. A simple method is the creation of a notebook or virtual folder in a shared drive or on a service like Dropbox, labeled "IRS Public Records." The file should include PDF copies of the annual IRS Form 990 for the past three years, the application, and letter of determination.

An alternative and acceptable response to providing copies is to make the documents widely available by posting them on the internet. They can be posted on the association's website or made available at a site such as Guidestar.org.

- **Antitrust Violations.** The Federal Trade Commission expects associations to have antitrust avoidance measures and policies in place. Orientation is a good time to educate the board and to document in the minutes that these measures exist. Again, if you don't have this policy, help the board develop one.

- **Conflicts of Interest.** Because the IRS asks (on the Form 990) if a policy exists to "disclose conflicts and how they are monitored on a regular basis," dealing with conflicts of interest is a topic for orientation. Potential conflict scenarios should be discussed, and members taught what to do if they have conflicts of interest. Many board members will have questions about this topic, and orientation can be the perfect time to discuss them and firmly state policies of the association.

- **Authority.** Directors may think a seat on the board gives them authority to speak for the organization. You will avoid confusion and conflict down the road if you delineate the lines of communication at orientation. Discuss various scenarios and solicit reactions. In the legal principle of apparent authority, it has been established that when a person appears to be an agent of the organization, the organization can be held responsible. So you want to be clear about who speaks officially for the association—it is usually the chairman or the executive director—and what to do should any board member get calls from the media. It is not wise to have board members making statements and representing themselves as an authority speaking for the association.

- **Values.** Organizations develop a culture of ethics and values that guide governance. Use orientation to discuss the board's values, such as transparency and diversity. If the board has not spelled out core values, this is another useful board discussion at some point.

- **Strategic Direction.** Orientation is the time to review progress of the current strategic plan. Update the new board members on the progress of the initiatives. If you don't have a strategic plan, discuss the need to develop one. Note: The discussion about the need for a strategic plan would be with the entire board, not at new board member orientation.

- **Partnership.** At the conclusion of orientation, directors should understand that their role is governance, not management. This concept might take some explaining, but the differences are important to fully understand. Many boards spend their time micromanaging the CEO when they don't know what their respective roles are or if they don't have a strategic plan to follow. They might start questioning or taking over duties of the CEO. One board I know of bypassed the executive director and hired a full time membership recruiter who had no background in sales, association management, member recruitment and retention, or member databases. The board then proceeded to direct the actions of this staff person with no involvement of the executive director. This kind of divisive action only harms an association. It takes the partnership of board and staff to advance the organization.

If you follow Harris' guidelines, the board's productivity will improve after you ensure that everyone is up to speed. Orientation is one area where you can make a big difference and it will significantly enhance how you are perceived as a leader. Providing this education will cement a good partnership in working with the board. It shows your expertise and clearly defines the roles of the board in relation to you and the staff.

There are additional ways that you can help your chair or chair-elect better understand his or her role and how you work together. Consider attending a CEO/elected leader seminar put on by your state association society or the American Society of Association Executives. This is a great use of time and allows the volunteer leader to hear from an expert what the role and responsibilities are. Another great resource for training is The Nonprofit Center website (http://www.rchcae.com) where Bob Harris, CAE, has dozens of free templates, including sample agendas for board orientation.

Mission and Strategic Planning

Every association should have a mission statement. It defines the purpose of the association. The mission statement is usually created by the board at a strategic planning session. A mission statement should be broad enough to last 10-plus years. If your association's mission statement has not been evaluated in the last decade, it might be a good thing to do at your next strategic planning session.

It is difficult to imagine a large corporation today without a strong mission statement that is a consistent message about itself. These declarative statements are repeated internally like mantras and broadcast to customers in the form of advertisements. Mission statements become the primary branding mechanism for a company. Likewise, the association board has to internalize the association's mission statement. They must live it. It guides them at every juncture of decision making.

The mission should be front and center at all board meetings, and staff should embrace the mission. At each board meeting, we print the mission statement on our table tent cards along with board member names. It is also printed on the top of the board meeting agenda in the header. Your strategic plan or initiatives should relate to your mission, and all new ideas and projects should be aligned with the mission. If a suggestion is made to do something that is outside the boundaries of your mission statement, view that as a red flag.

Do you and the board understand the mission of the organization? Is it clear? Ideally, a mission statement should be concise—one or two lines that staff and volunteers can easily remember and internalize. It should be the guiding principle behind everything they do.

One of an association's board's most important roles is to ensure that the association has a strategic plan, the road map that guides the work of the staff and moves the association forward. If there is a current strategic plan when you come on staff as the new CEO, determine whether the association is following it. Has everything been completed? Is the board discussing its progress at every meeting? Some associations do not understand how to create a realistic strategic plan and, therefore, spend time and money only to have it filed away because it was too daunting or did not capture important work to be done. If the association doesn't have a strategic plan, ask why and work on educating the board about why one is needed.

The Board's Role in Evaluating the CEO

One of the most important roles of the board is to hire the CEO, provide support, and assess the CEO's performance. Just as your staff wants to be evaluated and receive feedback about how they are performing, you need to ensure that you are getting appropriate feedback and guidance from the board of directors. Seventy-eight percent of respondents to an ASAE study indicated their organization had a written, formal process or policy for evaluating the performance of the CEO (Source: ASAE, Benchmarking in Association Management: Governance Policies and Procedures, 2011). If your organization does not have a formal performance appraisal process, you need to discuss this with your chairman. Do not allow the board to dismiss this responsibility. It is part of their duty as a board, and as the ASAE research shows, the majority of organizations fulfill that obligation.

The purpose of the evaluation is to set clear expectations and goals and then manage them over time. The evaluation should be a good discussion about how the CEO can improve as well as a celebration of goals achieved.

While most CEOs will agree this is an important duty of the board, there are actually some executive directors who brag that their boards don't set goals for them or give them evaluations. They tell me that the boards are very happy with what they have done and, therefore, no discussion is needed. You might think that practice is a compliment, but it is unprofessional. To me, it is shortsighted and could be disastrous. I know that if my association board did not have any interest in evaluating my performance, I would be concerned for my job. When you and the board have not agreed on what goals are set for you each year and how your effectiveness will be measured against those goals, then you are fair game when someone gets upset.

If no evaluation process is in place, here is another opportunity to work with the chairman on foundational structure and policy. First, there should be a board-approved process about when the appraisal is to be done and who does it. It should also note how the board is involved. For example, does the full board give input or just the executive committee? Usually you work closest with the executive committee, so often they do the review with limited input from the full board. However, some associations have an evaluation and compensation committee that handles the CEO's review. Whoever does the evaluation should report back to the full board with their report. There are a variety of ways to handle the evaluation, but be sure the process is written out and approved by the board, and then followed each year.

If the organization doesn't have an evaluation plan, its development could be part of a full governance process review, but it could also be developed separately. A CEO evaluation should be created in a thoughtful and deliberative way, perhaps with the immediate past chair leading a work group to develop the process and evaluation tool. Annual goals should be discussed and agreed upon by the board and the executive director and spelled out, and the results should be achievable with measurable, objective criteria. If you don't have the goals clearly defined, the evaluation could result in a lot of nitpicking and favoritism.

I remember talking with a new executive director about an unfortunate situation. The association held a board meeting one half hour after the annual conference ended (bad timing for a board meeting, in my estimation, as everyone is tired and ready to get home), and board members asked the CEO to leave the room but did not tell him why. When he was asked to return, they criticized the planning of the annual convention and brought up some mistakes made at the conference. It was awkward for the new executive director, who had not yet gained the trust of the board, and he was confused about what was going on. First, this discussion should have never been allowed to happen. It should have been shut down by the chairman. The chairman should have said, "We will discuss that at another time. If you have concerns, please submit them to me." But his silence gave the signal to the board to continue. Others chimed in as the executive director sat there, passively. Again, the chair did not step in. The executive director listened to upset board members saying how unhappy they were with his performance for the past six months. The snowball of criticism, made in haste, grew to be an avalanche of discord.

The truth was that this board had never evaluated any previous CEO and had never discussed having an annual evaluation with this new CEO. This became his on-the-spot evaluation because there was no evaluation plan, no trust, and a chairman who didn't know how to handle the situation. The chairman was unprepared, and the board's actions were clearly unprofessional. The executive director was fired two months later.

Another aspect of your evaluation is the employment contract. A contract is a safeguard for both sides. For the board, it helps ensure that the CEO is happy and will stay with the organization. For the CEO, it ensures that there are guidelines about how either party can get out of the contract. It also indicates whether the CEO should be paid for longevity and how much severance pay is applicable if he or she is let go without cause.

One CEO, the sole employee of the association, who had been employed for 18 years, was asked to leave a board meeting. Two hours later, the board called him back in and told him he was being let go. The board had decided to hire an association management company. The CEO did not have a contract. The board chair wanted to be fair with a severance payment, but the board members all got involved and had differing opinions, from no compensation, to one month's salary for every year worked at the association. The final resolution was two months' severance pay, but to get paid, the CEO had to work in the office during the transition. This example shows the importance for new CEOs to discuss a contract or at least a provision for being let go with no explanation or for cause.

Mary Logan, CAE, CEO of Association for the Advancement of Medical Instrumentation (AAMI), remembers two new CEOs who took positions without contracts. They were eager to get that first CEO position, so they didn't bring it up. They also took lower salaries in hopes of proving themselves and increasing the salary after the first year. But it was awkward. Without the contract (and without the knowledge that they needed goals, reviews, and performance feedback), they had no mechanism to handle the discussions, and they actually didn't know they could bring it up to the board. They thought they had to wait for the boards to initiate the conversation.

If you get a contract, the employment agreement will spell out the guidelines for an evaluation and how the contract can be terminated. It must be in writing, and Logan also recommends that a contract attorney review the contract on your behalf. An attorney herself, Logan had another attorney go over all the points of her contract with her and she found several areas that she was unfamiliar with, like an evergreen clause (meaning the contract renews automatically each year).

Since the contract outlines your compensation, Logan also recommends having the board use an association compensation survey (available from your state society of association executives or ASAE) as a benchmark or using a salary consultant who will do a comparison of the position to other similar-sized associations. The survey helps your board understand the salaries of other association executives of similar size or budget. Some boards mistakenly pay their executive directors based on what their industry pays (for example, paying an educational association executive director what a teacher makes). The salary survey also includes staff compensation and benefits for the CEO to use in budgeting staff salaries.

If you have taken a position without a contract, bring the issue up at your 60-day evaluation. The board may not be aware that that is a best practice. If you continue to get great reviews but no contract, take the time to research why a contract is a good idea for all parties and discuss that with the executive committee after one year on the job.

Board Meetings

To understand how the board is composed, refer to the association's bylaws. There should be sections in the bylaws that explain how people are elected to the board, what the qualifications are, what their duties and term lengths are, what type of meetings are held and when. Most state or national boards meet quarterly. In between board meetings, the executive committee usually has the right to make decisions on behalf of the board, and then those decisions are ratified at the next board meeting. Refer to the bylaws to ensure that this policy or others are spelled out clearly. If there is no mention of board practices in the bylaws, talk about how things get accomplished between meetings with the chair and make a note to self: Start looking at bylaws revisions.

Because of the involvement of the membership and the many fundraising events that volunteers coordinate, some local association boards meet monthly. How often you meet really depends on what is being accomplished at each meeting. It may be necessary to meet that often, but keep in mind that volunteer time is precious and should not be abused. If you are not discussing important issues that may or may not need immediate action at each meeting, you might consider reducing the number of board meetings. Again, check the bylaws because they may need to be revised before you can implement changes about how often you meet.

In associations, the decision-making environment is one of collaboration, involving multiple processes and layers of member involvement. Therefore, the length of time to involve and get things done is usually longer than in for-profits. This can add time to each major decision being considered by the board. Each association has a variety of committees and task forces that research and report to the board. The structure of the association is usually one where committees or task forces work on directives from the board, and final approval is given by the board. The association staff is there to assist, guide, and carry out the directives set forth by the board. Many senior staff also serve in leadership partnership in decision making. Work between the staff and the board at the most effective associations is very collaborative.

Although most boards meet four times a year, there are many options for board meetings, and they do not all need to be face to face. Some associations have a variety of ways to meet, since their members are located all over the nation or world and travel time and expense can be an issue. Meetings can be held electronically (conference calls, Skype, GoToMeetings format), but you do lose something when they are not face to face. Increasingly, communication technology is allowing boards to be more productive, so check your bylaws or policies to see what is allowed.

In recent years, the governance structure has been studied and challenged. When the book *Race for Relevance,* by Harrison Coerver and Mary Byers, CAE, came out in 2011, one of their considerations was to streamline structure or decrease the size of the board. Coerver and Byers argued that a smaller board allows members to be more engaged, nimble, and responsive. While I agree with their premise of streamlining governance, based on my experience there is no magic number of board members. Each association has different needs, and it is important to understand the culture of the association. Board representation can be very political. The size of boards varies widely. Some boards are large and composed of more than 100 members. In research funded by the ASAE Foundation and conducted by Beth Gazley, PhD, and Ashley Bowers that resulted in the book *What Makes High-Performing Boards: Effective Governance Practices in Member-Serving Organizations* (ASAE, 2013), the authors found the median size to be 15. More important to note, though, is that while they found board size matters some, board focus matters most. As a new CEO, you should tread carefully in the area of board reorganization unless the board brings it up as an urgent project to study. Take time to observe the board, whether all members are engaged and whether changes should be considered down the road.

Most associations have an executive committee composed of a chair, chair-elect, past chair, treasurer, or other officers. This smaller body can meet more often than the full board to handle business between board meetings. Unless the association is a local organization and members can drive to the office, many of these in-between meetings are held via conference call or videoconferencing. Again, their decision-making authority should be outlined in the bylaws.

In many associations, board members are elected to serve three-year terms. Officers may serve additional years. The chief elected officers may be on the board for three years, one as chair-elect, one as chair, and another as past chair. In some associations, the member serves as chairman for two years. Check the bylaws to learn the terms for your association's board members and officers. If there are no term limits, this is something to address, perhaps when you are doing a governance review and bylaws revisions.

It is important to have term limits. Too often, I hear of chairmen who serve in the top role for multiple years, board members who stay on indefinitely, and even past chairmen who are allowed to serve on a board until they die. Those practices invite problems. Their intent is continuity, and while it might be more efficient in the short term, it inhibits getting new points of view. What about bringing people to the board who can embrace change? Legacy boards tend to gradually descend to the social equivalent of a good ol' boys club. In the long run, association boards like these will stagnate and decline.

In conclusion, the board is an important group that leads the association. For some associations, the members may not be aware of what the board does or who is even on the board. But when an association is working well, it is often because the board is functioning well. When a board is not performing as it should, it is like little leaks in the dam before a collapse and flood. At first, issues appear as small mistakes, easy to forgive and dismiss as one-time errors. But they are signals of bigger, deeper problems. And over time, the frequency of these errors grows. The problems become dire. The membership witnesses them, and it doesn't take long before the entire organization is weakened, even to the point of falling apart. From the members' vantage point, it will seem sudden and strange—how did our association suddenly find itself in such trouble? But the writing was on the wall in the form of the board's inability to learn its role and carry it out professionally. Keep your association strong by working effectively with its board of directors.

CHAPTER FOUR

Undertaking the Role of CEO

An effective leader focuses on getting things done and making a difference and doesn't worry about getting credit. Defer credit to others whenever you can and stay focused on the end results. You will develop allies and support for future efforts and increase your chance for success.

    – John Sharbaugh, CAE
      Executive Director/CEO
      Texas Society of Certified Public Accountants

IN THE ASSOCIATION WORLD TODAY, almost everyone I know "lucked into" working for an association. Very few studied and planned to work for an association. Many people start out working in a staff functional position. For example, a journalism major gets her first job working on an association magazine or website. Some association CEOs had other careers before shifting into association management. In my experience, many people in associations were former lobbyists, attorneys, legislators, or legislative staff. Often, lobbyists and attorneys make this job change because they were employed by associations and helped represent them.

While there are some college certificates and degrees for nonprofit management, the pathway into the association management field is not clearly developed. Despite the abundant number of associations in every community in the country, association career visibility remains low. Awareness of the association profession is growing, but I think that because the association profession is not widely known, people are not sure about what skills are needed and many assume that being an association leader can't be all that hard. With some associations, especially those with small staffs, there does not seem to be a high level of professional regard for association executives simply because members and boards don't understand what we do.

Unless they have been in the position of CEO, most people don't realize all the facets of the position. A health-related association's long-time executive director retired. For 10 years, he and his chief operating officer (COO) had worked well together and the association (with 30 employees) was successful.

The board selected the COO to become the new CEO, and everyone thought that was a good idea. After all, he had been an excellent COO and knew the association.

But all was not rosy. Within the first few weeks of taking the position, the new CEO was already feeling anxious. Despite his extensive experience with the association, he hadn't realized how different the CEO job was. He did not realize how hard it was to juggle staff demands and the board's expectations or how a heavy travel schedule attending industry meetings would affect his productivity. Writing speeches and speaking to various groups was also new to him. It seemed that everyone wanted to meet him or have lunch with him, and he had no time each day to focus on what to do next. As the COO, he hadn't had the demands of members, the media, and elected officials requesting meetings; as COO, he had done a lot of his work independently. Now as CEO, he needed to get buy-in from members, and be collaborative—all very time intensive and stressful.

He also realized that he was "it"—he was suddenly responsible for everything. Before, he always had the support from his previous boss; now there was no one to take the blame if a mistake happened.

What surprised him most was the relationship-building required with the chairman of the board and the high level of teamwork that the chairman expected. It had not occurred to him that he would be discussing so many things with the chairman. That, itself, was almost a full-time job. He was worried about the fine line of building a strong relationship with the chairman and becoming too chummy (after all, the chairman was his boss), and he was not sure where to draw the line.

Since he had worked for that association for 10 years, he thought that the transition would be seamless, but that was not the case; there were so many new skills to learn. Among them was working with the board to determine if it wanted to make changes or to maintain the status quo. It was a lot more than he bargained for, and it could have ended badly. Fortunately, he began conferring with the past CEO about how to adjust to his new job and the skills required. Needless to say, he developed a new respect for the retired CEO.

The job does vary with staff size, but ultimately, you are the cornerstone of the association. You provide a path for the board and staff and members to move the association forward. You are part visionary, the face of the organization, taskmaster, bridge, and cheerleader. You wear many hats. Many times (especially with smaller-staff organizations) you are also the person setting up a meeting, the last person to leave, and the first one back in the morning.

Be aware that association staff leaders may be given varying titles, such as executive director, executive vice president, president, or CEO. They are basically interchangeable. It's merely a question of the traditions and preferences of the specific association. Years ago, the position of the principal paid staff member was called the secretary. As membership organizations became more structured and larger, and mirrored professional entities, they borrowed corporate terminology regarding leadership. There is no right or wrong here, but associations tend to have strong opinions on the issue. Generally, the larger the association, the more likely the title for the lead staff member will be CEO. I use the terms interchangeably: executive director, CEO, and president.

The volunteer leader's title also varies from association to association. They are usually called chairman or president, although if they are president, the chief staff leader can't be the president too. For example, I am the president and CEO of TSAE; the volunteer elected leader is the chairman.

Role of the CEO

No matter what your title (executive director, CEO, president), the chief paid employee position of an association can be a complex job. The very fact that you have a new boss (chairman) every year is hard enough, but you are responsible for such a large range of things: working with and coordinating staff, members, and leadership; finances; strategic planning; leadership development, and so much more. And all this is usually to be accomplished with limited staff and financial resources. The fewer the staff, the more hands-on work you may be doing or overseeing volunteers who take on those tasks. No one said it would be easy.

Association leadership combines a unique set of operational needs. Association executives must be tech savvy and understand and manage budgets and operations. If you have not worked in the industry that the association represents, you will need to learn its issues and the scope of what your members do. At its core, however, the association CEO position is a "people job." The soft skills of being personable and collaborative, having the ability to listen and negotiate, knowing how to motivate others, thinking strategically, and not expecting to be in the limelight are the skills that make or break a CEO. The politics of setting the right course and working with passionate volunteers takes finesse, political savvy, and integrity. The technical demands and knowledge required to be a CEO can be attained in numerous ways, but an inability to be a hands-on, customer-centric, personable leader foretells disaster.

While the size of the organization, vision, and culture differ among associations, there are similarities in the CEO's responsibilities. These include staffing, financial oversight, governance and strategic planning, working closely with a board, understanding the needs of the membership, building engagement, adapting to change, knowing how mature the association is, and overall stewardship of the organization. Each of these responsibilities is based on knowledge and the ability to affect progress. Let's take a look at these responsibilities one by one.

- **Staffing.** The CEO is an employee of the board of directors and is hired and fired by the board. Your role is to assist the board in managing the organization and achieving the organization's goals. The CEO is responsible for all business operations, hiring, training, and terminating employees. The board should not be involved in hiring staff other than the CEO.

- **Financial Oversight.** The CEO oversees the program of work and the budget, assists in the preparation of the budget, and is accountable for financial oversight. It is also important to understand that the operations of the association should be transparent: open, accountable, and providing members and the public with information.

- **Governance and Strategic Planning.** The CEO must understand governance structure of the association. This refers to the bylaws, board and committee structure, nominating and decision-making processes, and strategy (including short- and long-range plans that tie into the strategic plan). That is a tall order. All of these components make up the governance structure.

- **Working with the Board.** The CEO's main work is with the board. Therefore, you should be a board-centered executive. Understand that the work of the board is critical. Working well with your chairman is vital. The staff will take their cues from you, so don't fall into the trap of venting about the board to your staff. Likewise, the board should not be a good old boys club. Policies should be developed to ensure that a thoughtful, deliberative process is in place for leadership development and the board's nominating process. Understand how the leadership is selected and monitor whether it is working. Are you getting the best qualified people to serve on the board?

- **Understanding the Needs of Members.** The CEO needs to understand the profession or industry the association represents. If you were not hired from the membership, within the first couple of weeks on the job you should get out and visit the board members in their offices. Observe what they do and talk with their staff. I recommend that you call all the past volunteer chairmen, introduce yourself, and get their input about the association. Initially, the past chairmen likely will be flattered that you have reached out to them and recognize how important they are. Secondly, they always have opinions and observations. For many years, they were leading the association and they want to ensure that it continues to grow. The time that you spend on this outreach will be well invested. Continue to be out among the members as often as you can. This is where you will really get a feel for their pain points/concerns and how the association can help them. Many CEOs spend a lot of time at industry meetings, and this visibility is important. Keep in mind that you are not to upstage your volunteer leaders. This is their industry or profession, and they are the experts in their field. Take your ego out of the picture. Ask members, what does the association do really well? What makes a long-time member stay committed? What attracts new members to join?

- **Building Engagement.** Building engagement is another area where you need to review data and possibly be innovative if change is needed. Find out if the association has a lot of member involvement. Do members attend events or volunteer to speak or serve on committees, for example? Has a survey been done to gauge member satisfaction? Understanding your database and communications analytics will help you understand how many members are attending events or are accessing the website, online publications, and social media resources. Based on the participation of the members (and nonmembers), this information will be helpful in determining the value of the membership, as well as member engagement.

- **Adapting to Change.** Change is part of the job. In the last 10 years, several areas have changed dramatically including technology, volunteer time, competition, and generational differences. With today's CEOs, there is an expectation that you must be flexible, creative, innovative, and open to change. You need to be aware of outside influences and threats and work to ensure the association is relevant to its members.

- **Understanding the Maturity of the Association.** Associations tend to grow via cycles. First, there are new and immature associations. They have bylaws in place but may not have all the other structural components. Then, associations go through growth stages (getting members, building programs and policies, and so forth), and finally they reach a mature stage when the association is stable financially, has professional staff, follows sound policies and controls, and maintains members and programs. After that, associations continue to evolve as they go through evaluation processes, continually recalibrating their relevance to members. Knowing what phase your association is in is helpful to understanding the growth/renewal process.

- **Stewardship of the Association.** The CEO neither takes control of the association nor drives the agenda. Remember, it is not your association; it belongs to the members. Moving too fast, especially when you are new in the CEO role, can be a mistake. You must learn the balance between being patient but persistent about change. This is accomplished by having a thoughtful strategy and building collaborative dialogue with the board. Nevertheless, with the fast pace of change in the world today, CEOs are being challenged to question the traditional way of running an association. Within the industry of associations, there is already discussion about new ideas and ways to implement them, and there will be more changes to come as younger generations will expect different things from associations. In the past few years, many associations have been discussing reducing the size of their boards, ensuring younger generations are finding value in the association, transitioning from committees to work groups, empowering the CEO, getting rid of legacy-but-not-working-anymore projects (usually the elephant in the room topics), and dealing with the large number of executives who are retiring. Among the books that address these issues are *Race for Relevance* and *Road to Relevance, Knowing Y,* and others published by ASAE.

I often hear from new CEOs that their goals and priorities are unclear. They did not have direction from the board about priorities. There had been no discussion about what the board wanted done in the first few months.

A new executive director of a medium-sized health association (his first time as CEO) made drastic changes in the first couple of months after he was hired. He cut health benefits for the staff, discontinued staff meetings, created the board agendas without input, made legislative decisions, deleted several committees, and made large financial expenditures. He did not discuss the changes with the chairman, board, or staff. He based the changes on information he surmised during initial interviews for the job. After all, he reasoned, wasn't he hired as the executive director to lead the association?

This ambitious but naive leader did not understand the implied partnership that makes up association leadership or the culture of that particular professional association, where the leaders expected to be involved in every decision. Although he was the chief paid staff member, he never really understood how the leadership worked, and he didn't ask for clarification about priorities. It wasn't that he didn't listen; he didn't ask the questions in order to listen to the answers. His cardinal sin was being ignorant of the association's culture. He bounded ahead with his own agenda, and he was fired less than six months later.

Qualities and Skills of a CEO

Certain crucial attributes and skills are necessary to being a successful association CEO. Some of these are technical and require specific sets of knowledge and understanding. Others are harder to define. They fall into a category of behavioral skills. Both are crucial. For many association CEOs, satisfaction comes from the fact that there is such variety to the job, technically and behaviorally. There are different tasks to be handled each day. And every day is different. Others find the collaborative aspects of the job rewarding. For them, it is gratifying to work with members to make a difference.

Here is a checklist of skills needed to be successful as an association CEO. Consider it part of your CEO job description.

Technical

- Knowledge of association management
- Knowledge of board and volunteer management
- Development and adherence to board policies
- Financial, budgeting, and business management
- Project and time management
- Written and oral communications
- Data management and metrics
- Knowledge of parliamentary procedures
- Marketing, social media, and communications
- Analyzing, managing technology needs, planning for future technology
- Legislative or regulatory knowledge, if applicable

Behavioral

- Leadership and navigation
- Customer service, servant heart, non-egotistical
- Vision, strategic thinking, critical evaluation, innovation
- Negotiation skills and consensus building
- Decision making
- Global perspective
- Ethical character
- Relationship management
- Adaptability
- Measured risk taking
- HR knowledge, performance management, interviewing skills
- Developing culture
- Self-awareness/self-confidence
- Resiliency
- Ability to motivate others/engage volunteers

Soft Skills

If you are new to association management, a few skills are challenging to define, but equally necessary. They include the ability to understand and navigate board politics, board communication, governance, association market positioning, and volunteer management. Although people sometimes refer to them as soft skills, many a CEO has found them hard, indeed.

- **Political Astuteness.** As a new CEO, you should not only know how to run a board meeting but also understand who the players are around the table, what allies you have, what the sensitive issues are, and to whom people defer. How does your association board get things done? Keep in mind the answers might not be completely logical, but ignorance of the behind-the-scenes processes of the board can derail your best efforts.

- **Board Communication.** It is your job as CEO to ensure that the work of the board is shared with the members and any other interested parties. It is also your job to keep the board informed about issues and work being done between board meetings. A common complaint of board members is that they were not kept in the loop, whether the news was good or bad. Always communicate. Board members should be the first to hear of good news and bad news. Members call on them for information, so they need to be kept up to date.

- **Ensuring Good Governance.** You'll find that a good governance review is essential. You should review the bylaws and understand the nomination process, board orientation, policies, strategic planning, and all the legal documents, including your articles of incorporation and 501(c) tax status.

- **Understanding Market Position.** You need to understand where your association is today and where it needs to be in the future as well as how information is disseminated to the board, the members, and the public. Look at the association marketing pieces, including the website, magazine, and social media strategies. Do the public, legislators, and media look to this association for information? Just as a manufacturer markets its products, you market the association to members and potential members.

- **Volunteer Management.** Roles and responsibilities of work groups, event workers, focus groups, committees, and the board need to be clearly spelled out so volunteers can work together effortlessly. Giving volunteers responsibilities may require you to follow up to ensure the work is getting done to meet deadlines. Remember, volunteers are contributing on their own time after their regular jobs, so you are walking a fine line of encouraging versus nagging when something is not done (and then possibly stepping in and doing things yourself if all else fails).

I have spent a lot of time assisting new CEOs. It doesn't take me very long to recognize when new CEOs simply aren't cut out to work for associations. It is too bad, because they are often frustrated and do not really understand why everything is so difficult. Some failed CEOs criticize the leadership of the organization; others expect to be given more recognition; others do not know how and when to institute change; and others charge ahead without member involvement or input.

Some CEO's failures are not their fault. Some are hired and then flounder for a variety of reasons—no support of the board, no direction or guidance about what to do, no experience with staffing. Of course, if they come in without any training in association management, they are not able to offer guidance or suggestions to the board. It may take them a year or more to really understand all the nuances of association management and the board may be impatient. In such cases, those CEOs generally do not last more than one year.

How Does a Good Association CEO Act?

In 2011, Shelly Alcorn, CAE, principal of Alcorn Associates Management Consulting, interviewed more than 200 association executives from 501(c)(3) and 501(c)(6) organizations via telephone, asking questions related to association employment. (She used the appreciative inquiry method pioneered by David Cooperrider and his colleagues at Case Western University.) From the survey answers, she drew these conclusions about five personality traits of CEOs:

1. They are action oriented and love the fast pace, especially with legislative agendas.

2. They are organized and they create clear strategic priorities and clear financials. And they are focused.

3. They are relationship driven, and they continually connect members and show their passion for industry by developing future leaders.

4. They are future thinkers/visionaries, acting as change agents, researching future trends, embracing innovation and globalization.

5. They love helping people, and they help by offering educational programs, assisting members in time of crisis, serving as a sounding board, supporting career pathways, and developing strong foundations.

All these personality traits are useful in working for an association, and some of us have bits and pieces of each trait. Clearly there is no one singular personality type for an association CEO. That is the good news, because each of us brings our own personality to the table. What is crucial is that you match your strengths with what the group needs and what you have to offer and that you find ways to compensate for personality traits that you may lack innately.

Do you have to be a Type-A boss? A critical thinker? An organizational genius? A saintly peacemaker? The patience of Job doesn't hurt either, but seriously, no matter what your personality or skill-set, it is important to understand that from year to year, you'll have to apply your skills in different ways. Each year, you will be working with a new chairman. Depending on his or her talents and weaknesses, you will need to adapt to provide the association with everything it needs to succeed. For example, some volunteer leaders are not comfortable with public speaking or writing. If your chairman is required to speak a lot during the year (to legislators or regulatory agencies, at chapters or member functions, or to the media) you can hire a speech coach, help by writing presentations with clear messaging, or travel with the chairman and assist with the presentations. As for writing, there have been many years when I have been the ghost writer for the chairman's speeches and monthly messages. You do what you can to support them.

For now, think about your own performance and your strengths and weaknesses. Will you need assistance to get up to speed on some things? Identify your training needs and where you'll get that training. Perhaps a personal coach, members, or association consultants can assist you. When I joined the Pest Control Association, I knew almost nothing about lobbying. However, the contract lobbyist we hired took me under her wing and taught me a lot.

In thinking about your own management style and performance, be sure to consider how you will need to change how you work and manage, if you have not previously been a CEO. When you become the CEO, it is easy to take over and continue doing the work that you have been successful in doing in the past. In fact, it is important that you step away from those projects that you are strongest in (and could so easily handle). For example, David Gammel, CAE, executive director of the Entomological Society of America, brought a deep knowledge of website design and technology to the association when he was hired. He was tempted to get into the weeds and work on the website each day. However, he knew he had capable staff and after reviewing the site, he was OK with letting them do their jobs, allowing him to focus on things that were new to him and had a greater strategic importance to the association.

Developing and maintaining relationships is important to keeping and enjoying your job. You will find that you get to work with some of the most wonderfully successful, talented, kind, and engaging individuals in the world. Each day, you should wake up with the realization that you work with people who give of their time and talents to make a difference in their industry or profession, and they do it voluntarily. You get paid to do your job; as volunteers, they don't. Board chairs, in particular, often sacrifice a lot during their terms. I have been lucky enough to learn from 23 "bosses," and I try to learn as much as I can from them during their terms as leaders of the organization.

The workload will probably be overwhelming the first year. If you are new to the association world, you might find that office hours vary depending on when the members are available. In some associations, board meetings are held on weekends, when the members are not at their regular jobs. Some associations schedule early morning or late evening executive conference calls. If that is the case for your association, learn what it will take for you to be fresh and prepared for those situations. Do you need to leave work early, exercise, eat, and then find a quiet place to take late calls or rise early and arrange to be in the office before business hours? It may take a few weeks or months to figure out what works best for you and the association.

Likewise, traveling to meetings, conventions, and chapter meetings all are part of the job, and being out of the office so much can be stressful. Find a rhythm that is reinvigorating and sustainable. The last thing you need to do is work long hours every day, be stressed out about everything you need to learn and do, and possibly end up in the hospital. Yes, that does happen more than you would think.

Understand that you meet when your members can meet. Some educational association groups like to have their conferences during a long holiday when members are out of school. This may take some time to get used to. One association's annual meeting starts the day after Thanksgiving. The staff understands that they won't get to spend Thanksgiving Day with their families because they are traveling to the meeting site.

A word about balancing social situations: Many members like to congregate after meetings in the hotel bar or the chairman's suite. This is a great opportunity to get to know the members better or discuss an issue a bit more. If you don't drink alcohol, don't let that be an issue. It's no problem; just order a sparkling water or soft drink. If you do drink, limit your alcohol consumption even if the members are drinking heavily. A word of warning: Always be aware that your members are your bosses. Yes, wonderful relationships will be built, but do not get too comfortable or relaxed. Remain professional at all times.

And on a related note, be sure to talk to your staff about their behavior at association events. Are they allowed to drink alcohol if it's served with a meal? What about hanging out with members at the bar? One of the best pieces of advice I received came from Lou Goodman, CEO of the Texas Medical

Association. He said that he has a rule of drinking one glass of wine at any industry event and getting to sleep before eleven. He is responsible for a lot of things and knows he needs to have all his faculties about him should a crisis come up in the middle of the night or the next day. His job is to remain in good shape and keep his mind clear.

Starting a New Job as CEO

So you are new to the job. Congratulations! You are armed with the technical and behavioral skills you need, have the kind of personality that can gel with your association, and are determined to serve magnificently. What do you need to know to succeed?

Over the years I have made a list of miscellaneous practical tips for new CEOs of associations. They might not all apply equally in your circumstances, but I offer them to you as tidbits of wisdom, in no particular order:

- Active listening is critical, especially during the first six months. Listen more, talk less.

- Build trust with your leadership counterpart (chairman of the board) by spending time together, sharing meals, asking about family and interests, or playing golf or tennis. Always be available to the chair; provide information quickly when requested.

- Keep surprises to a minimum. If there is bad news, give it quickly and don't let the board hear it from anyone else.

- If you need to reach out for help, past chairmen are excellent sources of wisdom.

- Expect the unexpected; don't let it rattle you. The next problem is on the horizon, so continually scan the environment externally, and pay extra attention internally, especially to member politics.

- Prioritize the challenges and work you face.

- Be flexible.

- A big ego is not an asset, and you can't have one and be good in this job; be humble. Arrogance will turn the board and members away from you; instead, they want a leader to admire, someone who is generous and humble.

- Treat association leaders with respect and take every opportunity to take care of them. For example, ensure that your chairman is upgraded to a suite at your meetings. (Make this a part of your negotiations with the hotel.)

Greg Fine, CAE, CEO of Turnaround Management Association, offers some advice on self-validation when he talks about how it is lonely at the top, but not in the way he expected it to be. In his first executive director role, he was prepared to make tough decisions and knew not to second guess himself. He had an amazing group of other executive directors and CEOs who were available, willing, and able to provide insight and advice. What he wasn't prepared for was how lonely success could feel, and he recognized that he couldn't depend on others for validation of his success.

Within the first few months, Fine had resolved a years-long issue for the association, and when the board approved the solution, he was thrilled. At that same meeting, the board changed his title from executive director to CEO—another personal highlight. Later that evening, he thought about those two events, and while his close friends and family were pleased, he found that he couldn't crow about it to just anyone, certainly not staff. In the past, he had celebrated successes with his CEO, a great supporter of his. It was then that the reality of what it means to sit in the big chair came through. You are your own advocate, your own cheerleader. Enjoy your successes, big and small, and then prepare to move on. You can't rest on your laurels, or expect others to validate all your successes.

Remember, leading means knowing that you will make mistakes and acknowledging when you are wrong. Before David Gammel, CAE, became its executive director, the Entomological Society had been exploring the possibility of merging its conference with a competing conference. The preliminary reports were not promising, and Gammel initially dismissed the possible merger, agreeing that it probably would not work. But gradually, he began to research and gather more facts and eventually changed his perspective. He admitted that he had not initially done enough fact finding and that it had been a mistake to discount the idea so quickly. The merged conference is now a success, and he urges others to carefully review options and be willing to admit mistakes.

There may come a time when your boundaries will be tested. Kerry Stackpole, FASAE, CAE, president of Neoterica Partners and former CEO for several associations, relates an example of a fellow association CEO who had a meddlesome board member who directed all his energy to the association. Over the course of six months, this board member sent 850 emails to the CEO, often about insignificant issues. When board officer positions were being discussed, the CEO told the leaders that he would resign if this particular individual moved into an executive officer position. The CEO was willing to give up his job because he knew he could not handle a volunteer with this kind of behavior.

There may be instances in your career when you must decide if you will stand up and oppose what the board is doing. Your challenges may include situations involving unethical or illegal practices, poor leadership techniques, and bad or biased decisions. Handling these issues takes a strong leader and you should understand that your job may be at stake when you have such conflicts. Decide what battles you are willing to fight.

Know What You Are Walking Into

Some association CEOs stay in one organization for years, even decades. There are many benefits to such legacy leadership, but it poses certain challenges as well. For one thing, when there is a leadership change in an association, board members may have grown so accustomed to the previous CEO's way of doing things that they find it difficult to adapt to new ideas, even if the methods they have been using are outdated.

New CEOs, whether from outside the association or promoted from within, need to know what they are walking into. The concept of change may be less familiar in some associations, making it harder to navigate within its culture. The board may not be aware of how behind the times the association is or it may be perfectly content with the status quo. Other boards are ready to embrace change. Either way, you need to understand—and the board needs to fully agree about—which direction the association is going. Unfortunately, many boards do not take the time to evaluate where their associations are going; they just see an empty CEO position and fill it. You may need to be the catalyst to start conversations about change.

Imagine that you are walking into an association CEO role for the first time. If the search committee members did not fully assess the association's needs for the future, they may not have known who to hire. If they hired just the opposite of what they had, after a couple of months, they may not like the new hire, because they realized too late that they really didn't want any changes, and you were a change from what they had. So you may be out in a few months.

Similarly, if they didn't spend the time to determine what they were looking for, they may have hired you because you are similar to your predecessor. But if you are doing things differently, they may not like that either.

What are you likely to encounter as a new CEO? Below are nine scenarios. They are based on previous experience of the new CEO, ranging from no knowledge of the profession to being promoted from within the association. They also include the tragic replacement of a beloved CEO and the hasty replacement for an ousted one. As you read through each example, think how you would address the issues presented.

1. You were a member of the industry.

You are already a member of the association or profession and were hired because of your presumed industry expertise. For example, you were a dentist now going to lead an association of dentists or were a high school football coach hired to head a statewide association of coaches. What are your advantages and disadvantages as a former member of the association, and now the CEO? What are the advantages and disadvantages to the association? How are the expectations placed on your unique situation likely to manifest themselves when you're dealing with the membership, the board, and the staff?

Your professional experience brings a level of expertise that will be valuable when discussing industry issues. However, there is a lot more to the CEO role than technical know-how. Have you been in a top executive leadership role before? Even if the answer is yes, the peculiarities of association management will require additional training.

Time mustn't be wasted. It's important that you do the following things quickly: learn about association management, join the state and national society of association executives, and attend training sessions for association CEOs. Ask the state or national society of association executives for connections to other CEOs whose associations are of similar scale. Having a group of peers will be invaluable. Contact the executives of the other state societies in the industry. For example, if you are with the Gifted and Talented Association, there will be other state gifted and talented associations with CEOs. Ask these professionals to share samples and give you guidance in areas that are unfamiliar. The worst thing that can happen to you as a new CEO who was a member, is to assume that just because you came from the industry, you know how to run an association that supports it. Furthermore, you won't have a couple of years to learn the ropes; expectations are already high.

An additional complication of this situation is the likelihood that old colleagues will find it difficult to see you in a new leadership role. It may be hard to wear a different hat when serving as the CEO. Old colleagues may think that preexisting friendships will give them additional leverage and should override any policy or board decisions if conflicts arise.

2. You are completely new to both the industry/profession and association management.

You have not been a member of the association or worked for an association. Because both association management and the industry/profession are new to you, there is a credibility gap that must be filled fast. That is the top priority because without the trust of the board and staff, you will be ineffective. On the flipside, there is an expectation that you will need some time to develop skills. Both the board and the staff expect a learning curve. By being a quick study, you can gain favor and loyalty. You should do a lot more listening than talking during the first few months. It is data gathering time.

Time management tends to be a problem for anyone who is a complete newbie. There are competing forces at work: the association and the board. You should determine quickly how to allocate time between the internal issues (learning your new association's methodologies, culture, staff alignments, and so forth) and the external issues (reaching out to key constituencies, especially the board of directors). In both cases, nothing beats face-to-face meetings. You should spend time visiting board members on their own turf within the first two months. This is especially difficult for executives leading small-staffed offices. When you are hands-on, getting the work done every day, it is hard to justify time out of the office. But it is important, so consider if there are funds to hire part-time help, an intern, or a consultant to do some of the office work.

A big mistake that I've witnessed with this kind of CEO is the urge to launch key initiatives too soon. Don't try to impress the board and come out of the starting gate fast, before you have the expertise or the goodwill to implement new ideas. Instead, develop a strong grasp of your organization's capabilities first. And learn its limitations, too.

3. You are promoted from within the organization.

You're a new CEO who was formerly a staff member of the association. This is a trickier position than you would imagine. Having come from within, you have a wealth of knowledge for the first day on the job. Members of the association already are familiar and, of course, the staff is practically family. But is that a good thing? You have been a success story. That is why the promotion happened, after all. But as in any family, complex dynamics come into play as well. And much of your success or failure will depend on the degree to which the staff and board can recalibrate their relationships. Will the board give you a new level of attention? Politics, being strategic, and working with leaders will be challenges. Will everyone see you as a CEO or just as an old friend from the staff? I have heard many stories of painful transitions because, although prior experience in the association was helpful, the skill set required to actually run an association is different from what they expected. How can you address these problems?

Once you have accepted the position, the first day in the new job is critical. Spend some time planning in detail for the first day in the office. Hold a full staff meeting. Your remarks will set the tone for your new position, so plan carefully what you will say. On the positive side, you know the audience well, and the remarks can be tailored to address the staff's concerns and expectations in ways that would be impossible for an outsider to duplicate. Arrange for a volunteer leader to be there to set the stage and introduce you in your new role as CEO. This is the time for you to explain your vision, rally the troops, and unite them. Allay fears regarding upcoming changes, but be aware that everyone has questions about the future.

Politics come into play, too. Were other internal candidates considered for the job? If they are still on staff, what can you do to turn them into allies? Meet with them privately and talk about the fact that they applied and what their thoughts are about working with you, and see if you can develop a good working relationship.

4. You are replacing a legend.

You've been hired to fill very big shoes. When a predecessor was an industry icon—and this is often the case with a planned departure or retirement of an individual who has been with the association for years—you can feel overwhelmed with expectations. The organization has probably been well-run and is operationally sound. That is good news, of course, but it brings with it a lot of pressure. The task of stepping into the top role of an association that is already running smoothly is ideal. There is a lot of goodwill in the association, and it is in everyone's best interest to have a comfortable transition. If you have easy access to the predecessor, normally there are good feelings and the best of intentions to help you get acclimated.

The challenge here is how to best use these resources without disrupting the association's progress and impeding your ability to build confidence in yourself as the new leader. The association will be hoping that the transition is seamless, even invisible. That can actually be quite a challenge. You should determine how to best use the experience of the departing CEO. You'll need to determine to what extent the board is looking for a change. The balance between change and continuity is a question that needs to be addressed fully.

Some of the best transitions occur when the retiring/departing CEO is available the first week or two after the new CEO is in the office. One state association I know of had the departing CEO travel around the state for a week introducing the new CEO to key leaders in the industry. Then the departing CEO was available for phone calls or short visits for a few months. This way the new CEO has access, but it is not intrusive.

5. You're replacing a CEO who really doesn't want to go.

Sometimes, the board has agreed to allow the outgoing CEO to stay and assist for months, even a year. There are numerous drawbacks when there is an overlap of leadership, and as the new CEO, you should be on guard, especially if the outgoing CEO has not been given any responsibilities other than "train the new executive director." When a board states that it wants the new CEO to be "trained" by the former one, this must be a finite, measurable plan. You may need one week; someone else might like a month. However, having two bosses in the office is confusing to the staff and the members and can be awkward for you. By placating the outgoing executive who wants to hang around, the board does a disservice and undermines your ability to lead. Access and legacy knowledge are good; backseat driving and second-guessing are not. There can only be one person at the helm. On this, you must be gracious, but firm.

If the path for the retiring CEO is unclear but the board has promised him or her a consulting position, you should have a discussion with the board about the intent and purpose of this decision and how it will affect you. Explain to the board what you will be comfortable with in regard to your predecessor's role. If the decision to keep the former CEO on the payroll was simply a political thing to do, and the retired CEO is in the office with nothing substantial to work on, talk to the board about the situation. Agree on a final date of (early) departure; perhaps they will be "working " from home till the agreed upon date. You might want to host a "final day" party for the staff to say goodbye to the outgoing CEO or plan a luncheon away from the office.

Ideally, you will get along with the departing CEO. Best case scenario, he or she will be available to you, on call, as *you* desire. Keep in mind the retired executive offers a source of institutional history that might otherwise be lost if the door is shut and all communication ceases.

6. The previous CEO is not available.

For whatever reason (dismissal, disgruntlement), you do not have immediate access to the former executive director. Your first task is to gather data. This needs to be accomplished delicately, and it might take a while. Leadership or staff will be the best sources, but they probably will not be without prejudice and strong opinions. If it was a bad separation, staff and board may wish to vent, criticize, and gossip. It is tempting to wallow in such things and be the arbiter of blame, but a much healthier method is to acknowledge discord and then be professional about moving on.

You may find a lot of unfinished business in this type of situation. Be methodical about data gathering. Finding some information may be difficult. In some small staff offices, a list of vendors, banks, contacts, and passwords may not even exist. Document your discoveries and report them to the board. You may spend several weeks just trying to find information. It might take a year to fully uncover the goings on. In the meantime, there is an association to lead. In a sense, this lemons-to-lemonade situation can prove to stakeholders that you have the necessary skills to powerfully affect change.

7. Your predecessor departs tragically.

A beloved CEO has died. The first task for you as the new CEO is to foster an environment of closure. Tribute must be paid to the person, specifically regarding his or her dedication to the organization. Careful consideration needs to go into what you will say to the staff. Empathy is crucial, but even more important is bringing everyone together as a unified whole. This is a time to set forth a vision for the staff to continue their best work. A similar approach will be necessary at the first board meeting. Your recognition of the loss will help the board members realize that a new person is in charge, acknowledge their feelings, and pay tribute to the past CEO.

Any leadership change is hard. But it's even harder on the staff and members emotionally when the previous CEO dies suddenly, has been ill and passed away, or is medically disabled with no prospect of returning to work. You must recognize that emotions are raw, listen carefully, and be gentle. This is not to say you shouldn't move forward deliberately and firmly, but you should realize that changes you make will be perceived as having more impact than they would otherwise. Despite everything, high standards must be maintained from the start. Stress to the staff that performing well is a testament to the memory of the former leader. Staff members do no service to that individual if they expect less of themselves and fail to demonstrate their continuing commitment and capability.

8. You are filling a long void.

You've entered the picture after an extended time without a CEO in place or after a series of CEOs have come and gone. The assumption here is that the former CEOs were the problem. But is that accurate? On the first day, you may not have much goodwill. Staff and board members are likely to be tentative and wonder whether you will be yet another leader in the association's revolving door. Gaining trust will be a priority.

Initially, you need to discover the circumstances of the previous CEO's departure. This is eyes-wide-open time. Was the former executive fired or forced to resign? Are the problems endemic to the organization, or are they leader-specific? Is the association stable? Is membership declining? What is the situation with the staff? How are board relations? What is the status of its balance sheet? Hopefully, you reviewed these concerns and the financials during the interview process with the search committee. You cannot set a benchmark for progress without knowing—warts and all—how the association is doing.

It is entirely possible that the board is not fully aware of the complete picture either. There may be some issues that need to be resolved immediately. Maybe the bad news had not been shared with the board. Candor is a position of power. The trust proposition must really be accelerated here. The good news is that if everyone jumps on board and things get fixed, everyone wins. Stay positive, and keep the lines of communications open.

9. You are a veteran of a large association staff becoming CEO of a smaller association.

You have worked for a mid- to large-staffed association as a staff member, but now have been hired as the new executive director of a smaller-staffed association. You will find yourself struggling with time management, as you will need to know every part of the association, and in many cases, you will be doing the work of several people. You may be the CEO, but you also have to plan conferences, get dues notices out, make bank deposits, and buy office supplies. Where you used to delegate certain projects or be responsible for only certain areas, you will now find yourself handling almost everything. You probably won't have an HR or IT department anymore, and those two areas can take a lot of time. Bottom line, you will need to be more organized and prioritize your work.

On the positive side, you will learn so much more about the operations of the organization, and you will have ownership of so many programs. When the board asks about membership numbers, whether a certain person has joined, how many people are registered for the conference, or what articles are in the next magazine, you will know, because you will be working on those projects every day. You'll probably be outsourcing some responsibilities and will need to negotiate contracts and have working relationships with lobbyists, meeting planners, advertising representatives, IT specialists, and others who can assist with the tasks that may not be your forte so you can concentrate on your priorities.

Observations About Leading Successfully

No matter what situation you have walked into as a new CEO, you should realize that working with the volunteer leadership and members is, in general, the most time consuming, and potentially the most emotionally demanding, part of the job. It takes time to get to know people, support individual work styles, manage expectations, and determine and facilitate how volunteer and elected leaders can maximize their contributions. Diane James, CAE, executive director of the Greater Philadelphia Senior Executive Group, (whose resume also includes being CEO of several associations and working as an association staff recruiter) offers several observations about things a CEO can do to ensure success:

- **Develop self-knowledge, self-management, and emotional intelligence.** The higher the levels of these qualities a CEO possesses, the more likely the CEO will have his/her finger on the pulse of relationships and recognize the personality types evident in the organization. Essential relationship skills include active listening, maintaining confidences, and empathy.

- **Build a reputation for consistency of treatment, process, operational decisions, and transparency in decision making.** A climate of trust and fairness will create respect for decisions and deter individuals who may believe that personal power should guide decisions and processes.

- **Encourage board leaders or designate volunteer groups to deal with individual members who may be creating organizational problems.** Typically, members who create problems do so by violating policies, bylaws, organizational codes of conduct, or agreements regarding conflicts of loyalty. Some are simply individuals whose personality type is such that they truly have difficulty working in groups; have personal agendas in conflict with those of the organization or a specific committee, board, or task force; historically had a position of power and no longer have that role but expect to be treated as 'special'; are used to exerting individual influence or power; or represent a segment of the association with a distinct point of view intent on being vocal. Personal courage in dealing with one's professional peers is difficult and rare. Therefore, the association board and leadership must be given professional guidance; outside advice in governance, law, finance, and public relations when needed; and time to build consensus around controversial actions or decisions.

- **Build a strong partnership with the board chair and those who may become chairs.** The importance of being a good partner and helping the chair succeed cannot be overstated. There will be some chairs with whom this is nearly impossible. It may cost the CEO his/her job. Many skilled CEOs have experienced being terminated because of a failed relationship with the chair or a key board member who was successful in building a case for termination. Sometimes there was nothing in the CEO's control to change the dynamic. Like all significant relationships, the leadership partnership takes work, continuous support, and dialogue and yields best results when there is significant investment in building trust and collaboration proactively. Each new chair/board member is an opportunity to understand each individual volunteer's motivations and the communication and working style that best works with him/her. It is generally worth the effort to find ways to be accommodating to those motivations and styles unless the association will be negatively affected or its resources diverted improperly.

- **Know that understanding technology is now a key part of the experience of association leadership and that volunteers' comfort with technology will vary.** Provide training—in some cases individually—to key volunteers so that they know how information they need will be provided, accessed, and shared and how they will contribute their reports, insights, and issues. For those who travel and generally are participating via cell phones and mobile devices, systems must be readily accessible, centrally available, and reliable to avoid difficulty and frustration.

- **Do what it takes to keep your personal focus, balance, and wellbeing.** It's a given that there will not be enough hours in a day to accomplish everything you desire. There will be inevitable diversions that take even the most effective executive off track. In most associations there are more goals than time, money, and human resources available to accomplish them. Individual members or issues will always surface to distract even the most focused person. Creating and communicating priorities are essential. Seeking ways to delegate tasks is imperative. For some organizations, that might mean hiring or reorganizing staff but often requires engaging a combination of staff, volunteers, and interns. That, too, takes time, but will be well worth it. Just as we are advised on planes to "put on your own oxygen mask before assisting others," successful CEOs will take steps to maintain their physical, emotional, and mental health and to keep others clear about expectations, priorities, progress, and course corrections. Because neither the board nor the staff members are the CEO's peers, it's useful to keep a "kitchen cabinet" of trusted advisors, a peer group of fellow CEOs to meet or talk with, outside support systems of friends and family, and routines that ensure personal health. Take vacations. Have hobbies. Take regular time for enjoyable pursuits. Working nonstop creates only two known outcomes—burnout and resentment. Both lead to erosion of enthusiasm that eventually becomes obvious to everyone you work with. Managing your energy and finding ways to continually renew yourself produces the inner sense of enthusiasm that will continually reassure members that their leader is engaged and excited about the association's success.

- **Be authentic.** Anything short of authenticity shows. Being authentic does not mean saying everything that comes to mind. Professionalism still requires being tactful, sensitive, aware of the environment and audience, and using self-control to achieve desired results.

- **Understand the power of leadership.** Leaders who can inspire others, share and communicate a compelling vision, enable others to act, be trusted, and convey integrity consistently succeed. Lack of skill in almost any technical proficiency will be forgiven, if the CEO can inspire others to be part of the association through enthusiasm, vision, passion and integrity. As early as the initial candidate interview, association board leaders are impressed by these characteristics. They choose the person who will represent them well, will inspire members to be increasingly engaged, has executive presence, and will exhibit commitment to the industry/profession/cause the association represents.

CHAPTER FIVE

Working with Association Staff

You are ultimately responsible for the work of your staff. The board holds you accountable. With this in mind, your chance to show professionalism in all you do is magnified.

– Alicia Dover, CAE
Executive Director
Associated Plumbing, Heating, and Cooling Contractors of Texas

UNLESS YOU ARE A STAFF of one, you will be inheriting an association staff, or you will be hiring staff. Each association office is different, and each executive director has his or her own way of working with staff. One of your tasks in the first couple of months (and, of course, over time) is to assess the skills and commitment of the staff and determine what skills and positions you need for the association. Initially you need to review the performance of the staff members. Look at their annual reviews; what kind of track records do they have? Understand what they are responsible for and if they understand their job and expectations. Are they capable of doing their current job? Do they have the potential to adapt to new requirements? Are they eager to learn?

Your staff is your most important asset. It is your job to build the staff and set the culture in the office. Team-building is your job. Staff development is your job. Developing their future careers is your job, too. Unless you care about the welfare and development of your staff as much as you do about your own, you will not have a great team.

The staff is a reflection of you, and you want to ensure that they have the necessary interest and skills to do the job. That does not mean that they have to be perfect; quite the contrary. The wonderful thing about being a leader of a staff is the opportunity it gives you to watch them grow and learn. Over time, they will be able to handle more and more responsibility. You are the steward of their professional future.

Over the years, I have observed executive directors hired by associations that have inherited long-time employees who have not received any professional development for years, if ever. This should be a concern to a new CEO.

The industry itself is witnessing a generational shift. Adapting to new ways of conducting the affairs of the association is among the most significant issues we face today and you need to understand and assess staff skills. In addition, many offices have not kept up with technology. In some cases, staff may be reluctant to adapt to new computer systems or new communications media; however, younger staff can be frustrated if the technologies they use in their personal lives are not standard in the workplace. And growth of the association is hampered if it has lost pace with current methods of communicating effectively. If the board has not funded the upgrading of computers and infrastructure, this will be one of the issues you will need to address with the board. Of course, the challenges extend beyond hardware. Is your association effective in its use of emerging technology, social media, and digital communications?

In one office I visited, it was apparent that the office was still operating the way they had been 25 years ago. Clearly, the staff had not been given the tools needed to run the association in a contemporary way. There was no integrated association management system, large sums of money were being spent on three-ring notebooks (instead of downloadable formats) for all seminar attendees, rows and rows of file cabinets held paper membership applications and registration forms. The association website was lacking mobile interfaces, and many office computers and software had not been updated in years. Whether this was the fault of the board or the previous executive director, who knows? But if you come into a similar situation, it is your duty and opportunity to fix it. If board members are reluctant to invest in office infrastructure, you will need to start educating them and lobbying for resources. It is your job to give the staff the tools they need to complete their work efficiently.

As a new CEO, you may encounter long-time employees who don't want anything to change. Every organization deals with this issue. While tenured staff is usually a good thing, you will need to determine if they have the skills needed to move the association forward. Furthermore, you need to know whether they are willing to move forward. If you find they don't care about the association and are unwilling to learn new skills, you will have some difficult decisions to make.

Once you have begun your tenure as CEO, look to the professional staff to bring you up to speed. Review the staff personnel files and schedule 45 minutes with each staff member—maybe more if you have a senior management team. This shouldn't be stressful. Assure them that the purpose of the interview is to get to know every staff member and optimize your mutual goals. Tell them (and show them) that you are their advocate. Promise confidentiality, and ask questions such as: Is your current job description still accurate? If you had more money in your budget, what new things would you do? What are the challenges we face in different areas of the association—membership, board, technology, finances, and policies? What are the pain points you encounter in your job?

What are your department/job goals for the year? (Their goals should be in their personnel folders.) What kind of continuing education are you receiving/taking advantage of? Do you belong to a professional organization for continuing education? What skills do you have that are not being used? What do you like most about this association and office?

You should get a lot of feedback from the staff and you can begin to observe and note what changes are needed. It is also important to look at everyday practices that may need to be questioned. When David Gammel, CAE, arrived at the Entomological Society of America, he noted that each week he was receiving a written report from each staff person—a report on what they had done the week before and what they were planning for that week. These reports had been done for a long time, and the staff was just continuing to follow an institutional practice. After a few weeks, he recognized that he did not need these reports and, in fact, chose to use this opportunity to build trust within the staff. Asking them if they would mind not writing these reports (They were thrilled!) served as a valuable lesson that little things can be done to build teamwork, exhibit trust, and empower the staff.

Hiring and Firing Issues

Sometimes the board might indicate to you that staff changes are needed. This is a slippery slope. Keep in mind that as the CEO, you hire and fire the staff. While an informal board recommendation might be appropriate—and perhaps entirely accurate—don't allow board members to interfere in your staff decisions. Thank them for their insight and assure them that as the staff leader, you will ensure diligence regarding staff performance.

When I started with the pest control association and had an administrative position to fill, a board member suggested I hire his wife. I knew that would have been an awkward situation. With the job description in hand, I reviewed the skills that were needed for the position with him. I knew that his wife did not have the data entry experience or finance background that was required. Of course, he recognized that as well and agreed that she would not be a fit. It would have been a different discussion if she had been qualified—one about confidential member information and possible conflict of interest.

If you have been hired to make changes, you will want to take some time before making those decisions. If the board tells you that a certain staff member is "golden" and should never be fired, you need to have a candid discussion about that inappropriate comment and the situation. I know of a three-person association staff that had a long-time contract employee who worked on the trade show and sold advertising. She was in charge of bringing in the bulk of the association's annual revenue. While she was successful in obtaining the income and the board members thought she walked on water because of that, she was a toxic staff member. She blamed and berated other staff members publicly, was late on all deadlines (which affected the rest of the staff's workload and timing), and was a prima donna, coming in at odd hours and insisting that staff handle her important needs immediately. The staff resented her and did everything they could to avoid her. The new executive director was not sure what to do, and in the end, did nothing to address the behavior. He was new to the association profession, had never supervised a staff before, and didn't have anyone to talk with. He was most concerned that if she left, he would not be able to find someone to do that job and bring in the money. I assure you that you will find other people capable of doing any association job, that is, unless you pay very poorly or the organization has a reputation of poor management. Check with your local or state professional association of associations; most of them have job banks, as does ASAE.

Nevertheless, going through the process of letting anyone go is painful. Looking for new staff and taking time to train them are time-consuming responsibilities. But in the end, it is worth it. You may have some board members who will be angry if a favorite employee is let go, but hopefully, the changes will be so productive and positive that they will forget about it in time. Never think that just because people appear to be indispensable, that you should not get rid of them if they are not a good fit for you and the association.

If, after your review of personnel records and interviews with staff, you have developed serious concerns about the "fit" of an employee, you are better off addressing that issue sooner rather than later. Identify the best process for termination. Are there any protected class issues that should be considered?

Is there employment law counsel available? Do the personnel files support your plan with written document of infractions and concerns? Have you counseled the employee and kept good records? Your style of leadership and expectations may be very different from what they are used to. Give them time to understand your expectations, and if they cannot adapt, you need to make staff changes. Do it. Over and over we hear this lament, "I wish I had taken action sooner. This employee was bringing others down."

Greg Fine, CAE, CEO of the Turnaround Management Association, was a first-time CEO, and the greatest angst he felt going into the job was about the staff. After all, he had never been a CEO before, and the organization was facing some serious problems. He had been advised that not all staff would be happy about the change in leadership and some might even work against him. That could lead a new CEO to be paranoid and distrustful and also lead to micromanagement. He held one-on-one and group meetings with the staff and worked hard to praise what he saw was good. This team had been through a rough patch and it became clear that they were, for the most part, a group of highly talented professionals who needed to be empowered. So, he encouraged people to make changes in their own departments, supported cross-team collaboration, and approved staffing changes they wanted.

One of the first things he did was sign off on some needed staff changes that were delayed by the previous executive director. He instituted a weekly senior staff meeting where the group would engage in strategic conversations and develop a tactical team approach to problem solving. His goal was to create a cohesive team that could function in his absence based on a mutually agreed upon and implemented set of principles, policies, and procedures. It was made clear from the beginning that no department was an island and that senior staff were expected to share resources and ideas and develop strategy together. He also encouraged them to meet regularly with him present. This helped them gel as a team and also provided a needed opportunity to discuss all the changes that were being implemented. In addition, budget management became a team exercise, with each department head aware of not only how they were performing but also how their colleagues were doing. The entire senior team was responsible for ensuring the staff, not just their direct areas of responsibility, hit bottom line targets. This created a culture of teamwork and support.

He was committed to the long-term success of the team, and when it became clear that some individuals weren't a fit, the tough decisions were made.

But he didn't just terminate people; he also celebrated the staff that remained. After a month, he met with the directors who were there when he arrived, and he stated directly that "they were hired." In other words, he told them he would pick them for their jobs even if they weren't already on the staff. He wanted each person to hear directly that he wanted them on the team. They may have been hired by someone else, but now were firmly on "Team Greg."

Ask any executive director about personnel, and their advice is the same: "Be slow to hire, and quick to fire." No matter what size of staff you have, you cannot afford to have a toxic staff person. If it is not a good fit, it's not a good fit. Your staff will appreciate the fact that you want a cohesive, productive environment and that you considered the whole team rather than deferring to one, needy staff member. The staff change will bring a bit of drama for a day or two, but it's preferable to unending drama every single day at work.

Staff and Board Interactions

How does your staff interact with the board and members? This is an important question. Again, association culture and your management style will dictate their involvement. In some associations, staff and board members work together on projects and talk on the phone regularly. For them, those discussions do not need to be approved by the CEO. In others, no staff is allowed to talk with the board unless the CEO approves it. The board should realize that the association has wonderful professional staff, and most of the time boards are appreciative of the staff. But I have heard of some associations where this was not the case, and board members criticized the staff directly instead of taking their concerns to the CEO. Never let association members abuse your staff by yelling at them or embarrassing them. Never. How could you possibly win back a staff's trust if you permit such disrespect? If it costs you your job to stand up for your valuable staff, the job probably wasn't worth having.

The opposite concern is whether the relationship between staff and board is too chummy. And yes, there are many stories of staff dating board members on the sly. You need to be clear on what you will or will not allow. But policies can't be administered on a whim. You should have a written staff policy that spells it out clearly: The association does not allow dating and fraternizing between staff and members.

Staff Development

Give some thought to your first day in the office. You will want to have a full staff meeting and let them know a bit about yourself and how you like to work. Share with them key projects that have been identified as priorities by the board. Let them know your plans for the next couple of weeks—meeting with each of them, travel plans, routines, and so forth. If you have already determined that you are bringing in a new style of management, explain to them what to expect and how your style will be different. (Job descriptions will be written. Annual evaluations will be conducted. Weekly staff meetings will require attendance. Flex time, remote working, office hours, and dress codes will be evaluated.)

Staff teambuilding and professional development are part your job. Depending on your budget, you should consider bringing the staff together for a fun event within your first month at the association. Find out if anything has been done in recent years and what they might enjoy. Consider taking the staff out of the office for a half day.

Depending on the size and resources of your association, you might consider a staff retreat for the full staff or just the management team. It can include team-building events as well as discussion about the strategic plan and brainstorming. This could be done in one day at a location away from the office. Determine what you need to accomplish, and let the staff know far in advance. When planning, remember some are not thrilled with physical outings, some have dietary considerations, and some have family events that may interfere if your event goes beyond office hours. The goal is to involve and unite everybody.

Be sure that funds are allocated for the staff to learn and grow. Encourage them to attend seminars and conferences. One thing I hear regularly is that many staff members do not realize the association profession can be a career. They have a job to do every day, but they don't realize how their job fits into the overall work of the association. They may not know about the history of associations, how many associations there are, or the tax status of your association. Remember, they probably get blank looks when their friends ask what they do. Talk to them about their jobs and how they fit into the whole organization. Send them to an association seminar or course, including an Association 101 webinar or course. They will begin to meet other association professionals who do what they do, and they will realize that they work in a professional industry. Everything they learn should help them make improvements to their jobs and the association.

If you have a staff with directors or department heads, talk to them about how they are developing their teams. Greg Fine, CAE, makes it part of his directors' annual evaluations. He talks about ensuring all staff members attend formal educational programs through ASAE, the state association society, or a specialty course provider. He budgets for staff professional development, requires each staff person to take advantage of association programming, and celebrates professional accomplishments like the Certified Association Executive (CAE), Certified Meeting Professional (CMP), and advanced college degrees. Life-long and continuous learning should be the bedrock of the staff.

Office Culture

Office culture is an area often overlooked and not recognized until much later in a CEO's tenure. The look of the office, how people dress and act, and the collegial atmosphere in the office—or the lack of it—all reflect the office culture. The environment you want in the office is a byproduct of the priorities you determine. Situations in the workforce today have made us re-evaluate and change some of our work styles. First, you could have up to four different generational types working in the same office. Do they all know how to work with each other? Consider having a team-building session involving personality assessment or strength finders. You could bring in a consultant to talk through each personality or strength. The recognition of what each person brings to the table and how to interact with one another is invaluable.

Another change is the office itself. Many associations offer remote work privileges to save on office space, help cut travel time, or provide a different, quieter setting for focusing on projects. You must ensure that you have written eligibility requirements for remote working and policies in place to avoid the perception of favoritism.

Regular staff meetings should be held to keep everyone informed about upcoming events, and new information. You may have meetings weekly with the full staff or, in larger associations, with department heads; or departmental meetings may occur every week and full staff meetings only monthly or occasionally. One new association executive had come from an industry where he worked remotely and didn't have direct staff reporting to him. He didn't even think about staff meetings for the first six months until a staff member mentioned the need. If you have remote employees, there is an even greater need to have full staff meetings.

The Physical Office

You want to provide a safe and inviting space for employees. After all, we spend a lot of time together in the office. Do you have a lot of members, the public, regulators, or legislators coming to the office? Most associations I have visited have very few members coming to their offices. The exception is local associations, such as those involving realtors, builders, and contractors. Their offices are usually set up with training facilities or other resources and they see their members regularly. But even if you don't have many visitors, your staff works there daily, and they deserve a comfortable environment and updated working equipment.

If the office furniture is outdated and worn, talk with the executive committee or board about funds to update it. Just getting a fresh coat of paint and getting rid of "seen better days" furniture can make a difference. Some association offices reflect the industry and profession they work in. When you walk into the Texas Music Educators Association (TMEA) building in Austin, Texas, you know that you have walked into a music-related office. Tables made from recycled musical instruments appear throughout the office; instruments are the artwork; and there is a baby grand piano in the boardroom. The decor is a constant reminder that employees are in the business of helping people in the music business. The TMEA office has a large kitchen because the long-time executive director loves to cook and often prepares meals for the board members when they are meeting in the office. The culture in the office is one of family, common bonds, and relationships.

A Texas computer educator association I visited built its building around open, collaborative spaces, including gaming areas. They encourage staff to play games together. They offered stand-up desks to anyone who wanted one, and they have bowls of candy everywhere. There are several small meetings rooms, each named for the environment they want to create: creativity, solitude, and collaboration. It's very much in tune with how their members work and meet. They built a large training center where they hold regular training classes for the industry. In both cases, these executive directors spent a lot time thinking about their office environment, how to get the best from their staff, and how to create a welcoming setting.

Staff Policies

As you get settled in your new CEO position during the early months, take some time to evaluate the scope of staff-related issues. You should review existing and proposed programs with appropriate staff. Make sure you understand each department's purpose, fiscal impact on the budget, and concerns. Ask staff how their work areas are evaluated and what the feedback has been.

Study the existing employee handbook or employee policy manual to get a feel for what policies are in place. It will indicate whether the staff is following established policies. If the office does not have an employee handbook, add this to your short list of "things to do." Ask other association professionals if they would be willing to share theirs as a starting point, or check with your state/national association for samples.

I am aware of many instances when a new CEO realizes that a few staff are creating their own rules or made some up in the transition between CEOs. You may find that the personnel manual is out of date or that it is missing important information. Once you revise or create the employee handbook, ensure that everyone has a copy and signs a statement that they have read it and understand the policies.

Personnel files should be locked up in a secure place. Make sure you have the correct paperwork in those files including W-2 forms, written documentation of infractions or unacceptable behavior, background check results (if done), and salary information, including bonuses given. Pay particular attention to what the staff is being paid. If you are paying your staff less than your association peers are paying, you should show the compensation survey findings to the executive committee. If funds are not available immediately, you may have to wait for the next budget cycle. Your goal is to pay your staff a fair salary. Go too low, and you risk their leaving.

Salary is just one factor in a good workplace environment. The cultural compensations you set also are important to staff satisfaction. Do you offer a matching retirement plan? Health insurance? Dental insurance? Consider paid time off instead of the traditional paid and sick days so that employees have more flexibility. Think about variable office hours if that would benefit employees with children or long commutes. Look at your policy on bad weather. Do you close the office if the schools close? Do you have a relaxed dress code on days when meetings are not held? While association salaries may not match corporations, sometimes the perks of time off are a huge consideration to your staff. For example, some associations close on Friday afternoons in the summer, and many educational associations have the same vacation schedules as their members. So if teachers have extended holidays (spring break, Christmas), so does the association staff. It's hard to put a price tag on that.

Fraud Warning

You must ensure that all steps are being taken to mitigate any possibility of fraud by staff or volunteers. I am sorry to say that nonprofits in general have historically had problems with fraud issues. The section on finances in Chapter Eight will explore the problem in detail, but be aware of any staff member who does not take vacations, and has access to cash. Think about your conventions or seminars where people may pay with cash, or small staff situations where separation of duties is difficult. These are potential red flags. Check to see whether any staff members have association credit cards. You will need to determine if they are needed, but more importantly, who is approving and monitoring the card usage.

One association gave senior directors credit cards with little direction about what they were authorized to charge on them. All the staff members used them for association travel and hotel expenses, but they also used them for everyday personal expenses (gasoline, groceries, home electricity payments, and clothes). It added up to a substantial amount of money, and the association had paid those bills for a long time. Until a new CEO was hired, no one had been reviewing the bills and ensuring that those charges were billed back to the employees. Several of the employees who misused the credit cards left the association soon after the new executive director arrived, and the association never got that money back.

You want people on your staff that you can trust to do their jobs well and who have the highest ethical standards, but you also need to ensure that procedures are in place to mitigate fraudulent opportunities. Maintain an open door so that staff can talk to you about concerns, and be fair when dealing with all staff. As the CEO, help the staff realize their potential, and be supportive. Over time, you will lose staff members. Some will move on to further their careers. When that happens, you will realize that you have provided them with the opportunity to learn and progress.

CHAPTER SIX

Embracing Good Governance

Always tell the truth and be transparent. Providing bad and/or good news to a board of directors establishes trust and respect.

– David DuBois, FASAE, CAE
President and CEO
International Association of Exhibitions and Events

WHILE MANY ASSOCIATIONS ARE WELL-GOVERNED, professionally managed, and doing a wonderful job, some organizations do not understand the importance of good governance and how poor governance procedures can lead to dysfunction. Over the years, I have heard about and witnessed numerous dysfunctional boards and observed CEOs who are struggling with their boards. Working with the board is the largest source of aggravation for many CEOs, followed closely by staffing issues. Working well with the board is also a huge factor in the CEO's success—and professionally fulfilling for those who are good at it. But why do CEOs run into frustration in working with their boards? Is it a problem of the CEO, the board, or the staff? When I delve into the situations more, it almost always turns out that processes were not in place; policies were not well defined or properly followed. Members had not been educated about their roles as volunteer leaders. Most issues could have been avoided if the proper governance structure had been in place. In my experience, governance is where a lot of things can go wrong.

Every association board is different, with personalities and politics playing out in different ways. I have heard of rogue board members engaging in strange and frightening behavior—and this is no exaggeration—including guns being drawn and tires being slashed. And though not nearly as scary, there are always examples of board members making a CEO's life miserable by micromanaging, spending board time questioning the tiniest line items in the budget, or questioning why certain work is being done. Dysfunctional boards, whose members do not understand what they were elected to do, may start to make up rules or insist that new projects be started that have no funding, no plan, and no alignment with the strategic plan. Good governance can minimize, if not prevent, these challenges. To protect everyone, the governance structure needs to be strong, understood, and followed.

Governance involves ensuring that there are professional processes that help delineate decision making and ensure that the organization is well managed. ASAE has published several books about good governance practices, including *What Makes High-Performing Boards: Effective Governance Practices in Member-Serving Organizations; The Will to Govern Well: Knowledge, Trust, and Nimbleness;* and *From Insight to Action: Six New Ways to Think, Lead, and Achieve,* which builds on the knowledge-based model.

While some governance challenges, including taking actions outside the mission and strategic plan, board orientation, and the CEO evaluation were discussed in Chapter Three, there are a few other issues that regularly cause problems with the board. They include board members' not being adequately vetted in the recruitment and nominating process, conflicts of interest and personal agendas, and poor board self-evaluation processes.

Board Recruitment

Recruitment consists of many parts: ensuring that you have spelled out the qualifications needed so that you are attracting the right people, development of job descriptions, understanding term limits, and the nomination process and election. All these components would be part of a governance review. The CEO and volunteers work together to create the board and officer job descriptions, the nomination and election processes, and any bylaws changes that are needed. The CEO should gather information or tools on best practices for each area and be prepared to lead the volunteers in making these changes.

There needs to be thoughtful discussion about the makeup of the board, what kind of board you need for your organization. Spell out what characteristics you want on a board: integrity, wisdom, independent thinking, humor, visionary mindset, business knowledge, experience as a volunteer, fairness, and willingness to challenge. By looking at the current board, you can start to clarify what characteristics and skills are needed in the future.

Do you need members with years of leadership experience, people with certain content expertise, fundraisers, high-profile members, and/or association supporters? Do you need a mix of some who have this experience, balanced with others who are just learning the ropes?

Associations change over time, and that calls for periodic review, fine tuning, and sometimes a major overhaul of the governance structure. Organizational performance, like human performance, is cyclical in effectiveness and should be reviewed and renewed as it evolves. To undertake this periodic review, consider setting up a governance review task force to study the methods and systems under which the organization operates and determine if changes or new methods are needed.

Associations tend to grow in cycles, and each phase may require different skills sets from board members. First, there are new and immature associations. They have bylaws in place, have founding board members who are passionate about the new organization, and are building structural components. Then associations go through growth stages (getting members, building programs and policies), and finally, they reach a mature stage when the association is financially stable and has a professional staff, sound policies and controls, members, and programs. After that, associations continue to evolve as they go through evaluation and reinvention, continually recalibrating their relevance to members; therefore, continually evaluating board needs is important.

Your association's bylaws are always a good place to start when reviewing the governance structure that affects your board recruitment. As a new CEO, you may find that the association has not been following the bylaws or circumstances have changed, making portions of the bylaws obsolete. The process of revising bylaws is an ideal time to look at the makeup of the board because most board structure changes require amendments to the bylaws. A task force should be created to review the makeup of the board, including qualifications, requirements, and responsibilities of board members and the nomination process, and to make sure they are spelled out and that they meet the association's current needs. The CEO will be intimately involved in this process, often asking why things are done a certain way and offering examples from other organizations.

Just as the CEO has a job description, so should the board, officers, and committee members. Your bylaws should provide guidelines for each. Each year, you should review everyone's duties as part of board orientation. It is surprising how many board members have never been advised of their responsibilities, roles, and expectations. Each year, it is also necessary to clarify the relationship between the CEO and board. As new board members come on, old ways of governance disappear. This can be good or bad. You must prepare for both by regular evaluation.

You may wonder how to select the best candidates for your board. Just as the selection of a CEO takes time and deliberation, the selection of a board member should be given the same degree of scrutiny. When determining the composition of the board, diversity, tenure, and reputation should be considered.

There is no consensus about how large a board should be. Arguments for having a smaller board include ensuring that board members are engaged and involved. Arguments for having larger boards usually have to do with tradition and politics, usually over financial contributions, geographic representation, and even familial representation. I've seen one association that lets members stay on the board until a family member replaces them and another that allows any member who wants to pay the suggested price be a board member. Since 2011, many boards have had the discussion about board size after reading *Race for Relevance* by Harrison Coerver and Mary Byers. (This is recommended reading, by the way.) The correct board size depends on what works best for each organization; however, the flexibility of a smaller board is certainly enviable in today's fast-changing environment.

The Need for Diversity

Diversity on your board is more than a trend. It is a necessity. Proportional representation means structuring your board to reflect your membership. This means having a proportional ratio in areas of gender, race, economics, experience, and even geography. If you want to be relevant to your organization, your board should proportionally reflect the membership of your organization.

Notice that I use the term "proportional." Proportionally balanced is not the same as equally balanced. If your membership is 90 percent men and 10 percent women, then strive to make sure at least 10 percent of your board members are women. This applies similarly to all demographic categories. If 90 percent of your membership is urban and 10 percent is rural, then strive to include someone to represent the 10 percent rural contingency. But that doesn't mean you should give anyone a larger presence on your board just because they represent a larger "geographical footprint." Their representation should reflect the percentage of the membership they represent. This is diversity, proportionally based.

Once elected as members of the board, board members do not represent any single constituency. They may be more knowledgeable in a particular area, but their responsibility is to the association as a whole. Many board members have never been taught this rule. They continue to vote for their district or chapter instead of what is best for the association as a whole. And even worse is when they disagree with a decision of the board, go back to their local chapter or region, and tell everyone that they were against it even if the rest of board voted for it, creating an us-against-them scenario.

Create a matrix to review who is currently on the board and determine if voids exist. Gathering the following information will give you a good picture of the board makeup: age, sex, size of company they work for, type of membership, years in the business, when terms expire, geographic representation, credential or degrees, ethnicity, board experience, and years as an association member. If you find you have all males of a certain age, you probably don't have a diverse board. When the board development or nominating committee starts to look for candidates, they can refer to this matrix to see who is going off and what qualifications might be needed in the next board members.

Board Nomination Processes

The nomination process can be done different ways. Some associations extend informal invitations to those they have identified as desirable; others have regional affiliates or chapters submit candidates; others use a nominating committee process; and still other associations make running for the board a huge political race. I am not an expert in all these varieties, but I do know that the process should be clearly specified in the bylaws and that the entire process should be transparent.

Here is an example using TSAE's annual nominating plan:

1. Bylaws clearly spell out requirements and qualifications of candidates for the board, and how to apply.

2. Bylaws spell out the nominating committee duties, the timeline of when nominations are sought, when members vote on a slate of candidates suggested by the board, and individuals are put on the open ballot for vote. They also explain what to do if someone wants to protest a candidate and how to submit a petition against a candidate. TSAE's nominating committee selection is spelled out in the bylaws so that board members cannot be nominated by one person or a small clique.

3. A call for nominations is sent to members, put on the website, and publicized in newsletters and email. The notices spell out how many open positions there are, qualifications, expectations, how to apply, and the timeline for applications and voting.

4. Candidates' applications are submitted on a template that is populated with specific questions that all candidates must answer. The nominating committee then reviews all the applications and ranks them.

5. The nominating committee narrows applicants down, and finalists are asked to attend a face-to-face interview with the nominating committee.

6. The nominating committee rates and makes the selections and that slate is presented to the board for final approval, along with the terms for each candidate. The slate is then sent to the membership for approval with a deadline and if no one objects, they are nominated by acclamation.

Having a membership that does not understand how you get on the board is a concern. Making public the timeline, the number of positions open, how many board meetings there are, time requirements, who is eligible to run for a position, qualifications, how they apply, and the interview process are all important to let the members know how they can get involved.

A best practice model is one where each board member is elected for a set term (usually three years), with staggered terms so that each year a certain number rotate off, and new members are seated.

When I hear some CEOs say that they can't ever find anyone to serve on the board, so the same people just continue to serve, it raises a concern in my mind. There is a bigger problem at the root of that issue: Could the requirements be too rigorous? For example, do candidates have to have been members of the association for a certain number of years (maybe 10) and have served on various committees before being considered? Could the board be perceived as an old boys' club? Do candidates have to make large financial contributions to serve on the board, thus cutting out people who can't afford that? Does board service require an inordinate amount of time? Candidly scrutinize the board process, perhaps including a survey, to determine the root problem of why members are not interested in serving.

Conflicts of Interest and Other Policies

Well governed organizations have thoughtful policies that deal with board practices and serve as guidelines. One policy that is of great importance to many boards is understanding conflicts of interest.

In an association where I was on staff a board member suggested that all board and committee travel be booked through a travel agency instead of members taking the time to individually contact the airlines and hotels. While that seemed like a good suggestion (and the board approved the recommended travel agency), the member making the suggestion did not disclose that his wife was a co-owner in the travel agency. It came to light about a year later, but because the board members were happy with the service, they continued the agreement. Technically, the first wrong was the board member's failure to disclose the relationship (and monetary gain to be made). If you think the board was wrong to continue the relationship, I would agree. But full disclosure was made at that later time, so one could argue that the board made a fully informed decision in continuing the practice. This association did not have a conflict of interest policy, and had there been one, the outcome and discussion might have been different.

Policies should be in place to protect the board and reflect the actions of prior boards. Knowing what policies have been passed by previous boards is important information for board members. Policies help to interpret and frame the bylaws as well as spell out what board members can and cannot do. Policies made by the board are captured in the minutes. To make policies easy to reference, copy the policies from the minutes and include them in a policy manual, listing each policy by department (financial, governance, and so on) and including the date when the policy was made. Add the policy manual to the orientation session for the board and review the key policies.

In 2002, the Sarbanes-Oxley Act was enacted by the U.S. Congress to protect shareholders and the general public from accounting errors and fraudulent practices in enterprise as well as improve the accuracy of corporate disclosures. It generated a lot of discussion among nonprofit organizations and their boards, but does not currently apply to nonprofits. However, as a best practice, many associations voluntarily subscribe to its tenets. So, what do you need to know about Sarbanes-Oxley?

With a couple of exceptions (whistleblower protection and rules against destroying documents, both of which are described below), the procedural guidelines in the Sarbanes-Oxley Act apply only to publicly-traded, for-profit companies. So, with those two exceptions, Sarbanes Oxley doesn't apply to nonprofit operations.

Sarbanes-Oxley prohibits publicly traded companies and nonprofits from retaliating against whistle-blowers. Anyone who reports impropriety in a company's financial management or employment practices is protected. A company can't fire, demote, suspend, harass, or fail to promote any employee who reports improper activity, even if the report turns out to be unfounded. The only requirement is that the employee had a reasonable belief or suspicion that wrongdoing had occurred at the time he or she made the complaint.

In addition, Sarbanes-Oxley makes it a federal crime for publicly traded companies and nonprofits to intentionally destroy internal documents in order to prevent them from being used in an official government proceeding or investigation. Sarbanes Oxley does not prohibit all document destruction, but it does highlight the need for document-retention policies. Any organization exposed to a government investigation or enforcement proceeding should be very careful about destroying internal documents.

Besides those two policies, it is important to understand that while the law does not require them to do so, many nonprofits may still want to follow the guidelines within Sarbanes-Oxley because they represent good management practice.

In a broader context, and to mitigate potential risks, boards should discuss and approve the following policies:

- **Code of Ethics.** Code of high standards in ethical behavior that applies to the board, members, management and staff.

- **Conflict of Interest.** Ensuring the board and staff fully disclose any conflicts. A wise board will discuss some examples during orientation or a board meeting. For example, if a board is discussing the possibility of creating a credentialing program and a board member serves on the board of another organization that has a credentialing program for the same audience, that involvement needs to be disclosed to the board. The board will then discuss openly if the situation is a conflict of interest and if the board member needs to abstain from discussion and/or voting.

- **Antitrust.** This policy prohibits contracts, combinations, or conspiracies in restraint of trade. By their very nature, associations are a "combination" of competitors, so one element of a possible antitrust violation is always present. Any action by an association that unreasonably restrains trade could constitute an antitrust violation. The board needs to be reminded to avoid agreements on prices, fees, and boycotts. Another example is that membership decisions must be based on published eligibility criteria (bylaws) and nothing else. And finally, when it deals with access to member benefits, you must offer benefits that are essentially the same, or nearly the same, to nonmembers. But, yes, you can charge a higher price to nonmembers.

- **Whistleblowers.** This policy is in place so that any staff or board member can raise issues about the organization's ethical or financial practices. The policy should clarify how to raise such issues and how to prohibit retribution for raising them.

- **Document Retention and Destruction.** A document retention and destruction policy identifies the record retention responsibilities of staff, volunteers, board members, and outsiders for maintaining and documenting the storage and destruction of the organization's documents and records. IRS Form 990 asks whether an association has a policy for document retention and destruction. You want to be able to check "yes" on that form. A sample list of records that you keep is in Chapter Eight.

Keep in mind that policies are not procedures. Procedures are administrative responsibilities, developed by staff. For example, procedures identify steps for backing up computer data or for processing a new member.

Board Evaluation

Board members should be allowed to give feedback for improvement of the board meetings so they can feel engaged and part of improving the board. After each board meeting, distribute a survey to board members asking about things such as pre-meeting communications, agenda and background materials, format, content and discussion, and strategic discussion. Have participants rate their advance preparation for the meeting (Did they read the board materials?) and their participation during the meeting. For many association boards, this exercise can be an eye-opening experience. It is valuable feedback for the CEO and the chairman, who review them and make changes, if appropriate.

The surveys may point out if you have not provided enough background material or allowed enough time for discussion. Some of the simple suggestions we've received and implemented at TSAE included sending an Outlook calendar note to board members for each scheduled board meeting, having name tent cards for the staff, and emailing a duplicate agenda separate from the board packet so they can toggle back and forth on their laptops during the meeting.

CHAPTER SEVEN

Working with the Board

Pick your battles carefully by giving considerable thought to which ones are worth taking on immediately and which ones you're better off putting on hold until you have built ample trust and credibility within and sufficient knowledge about the organization.

> – Ed Leach, CAE
> Executive Director
> National Institute for Staff and Organizational Development

WORKING WITH AN ASSOCIATION BOARD is not easy, as you can gather by having read the chapters to this point. Whether in the job one year or 25 years, all association executives will go through some difficult times in working with the board or with particular board members.

George Allen, CAE, has been the executive vice president of the Texas Apartment Association for 25 years. When other association leaders talk about such long-tenured chief paid executives, they wonder how anyone "survives" all those years. The word survival has always seemed a bit strange, as though we are in a fight with our volunteer leaders. Yes, there are some years when working well with a chairman or the board is a struggle, but as Allen explains, "Serving the board for that many years boils down to knowing which issues are most important to stand up for, when is the best time to make a stand and what resources you can tap to help you make your case. Successful executives must have a capability to bite their tongue on occasion when in disagreement with the leadership, but have a willingness to speak up and be heard when needed to keep the leadership focused on key goals and the association's core mission. But always remember that the association belongs to the members, not the staff, and nothing is more important than what is in the best interests of the members."

Tips for a Successful CEO/Board Relationship

Working with a board offers unique challenges. One of the biggest differences between associations and corporations is that association volunteer chairmen change every year (or two) and the board turnover is ongoing. With corporate boards, members can stay for a long time. Usually association boards have term limits, so there is an annual churn of board members coming on and going off. Your job, as the association CEO, is to assist the new chairman and the board and to provide continuity. Unfortunately, sometimes a CEO abuses his or her power, taking over, keeping the board in the dark, and just running the show no matter what the board wants. What you should want to create is a partnership, a collaboration to move the association forward.

It is important to get to know and partner with your chairmen and understand how to work with them. Some years are more rewarding than others. However, that is only for you to know. Your job is to work well with every chairman, every board, every year. What's interesting is that past chairmen carry a lot of weight even years after they have left office. If you have had a successful year during their chairmanships, you will have allies to call if you are unsure about something and want advice. They will turn out to be your best supporters. Conversely, if you have a poor working relationship with the chair, that discomfort can fester for years, and cases for dismissal have stemmed from such situations.

Your goal is to be transparent in all you do. This is especially important if there has been a mistake. You need to be willing to take responsibility for any mistakes and not blame others.

In working with the board, disagreement can often be beneficial, but be prepared if you are criticized. If the board (or a board member) is critical of your work, do not get defensive. Ask for clarification and provide information, or ask them more questions to get to the root of the concerns. It is easy to get caught up in the heat of the moment. What I'm suggesting is that professionalism takes the heat out of such confrontations.

Your job is to help move things forward. Depending on the life cycle of the association, help the board understand where the organization stands. Is it mature and needing to evaluate long-standing (and perhaps outdated) traditions? Is it in a startup mode and needing to build resources, members, and structure? Perhaps it is in a holding mode and needs to get ideas to change things up, to attract younger members, merge with another group, or pursue a different focus or mission. For each cycle—and in the course of your leadership career, you may see all of the above—you can discuss the challenges with the board and develop plans. These discussions can be enlightening and foster great input and dialogue.

When it comes down to building the foundation for success with a board, however, it boils down to trust. Trust among you, the board, the members, and of course, the staff. But you must start with the chairman, the executive committee, and the board.

When you do not feel and see the support of the board, when there are lots of side bar conversations without you, when they are not answering your questions or your phone calls, when you cannot seem to do anything right in their eyes, when they are not listening to you and in fact, are meeting without you—those are all red flags that they don't trust you. Very simply, if you don't have their trust, you won't last very long.

So how do you build trust? Sometimes, CEOs are given trust when hired and then blow it by not communicating, not listening, or not doing the work the board asks for. Other times, the CEO has to earn trust and it might take a long time to build to a solid relationship. When the past chairmen seek you out to give you information, when the board endorses and supports your ideas, when you can talk candidly with the chairman, when there is collaboration going on between you and the board, you have a trustful environment.

Starting Off on the Right Foot

As soon as you have been hired, one of the best things a board can do is set up an on-boarding plan for yourself. This plan should entail getting you informed and involved the first week or two. If there is an outgoing executive director, the plan would outline how he or she can assist you for a certain amount of time, introducing you to members and key contacts (regulators, lobbyists, CPA, auditor), helping to review the status of projects and events, and getting you set up at the office. If a predecessor is unavailable, board members can serve as a similar resource. Working with engaged volunteer leaders following an outline of what things you'll learn in the first two weeks is the best situation. If an on-boarding plan does not exist for you, it is up to you to request this kind of orientation.

According to many surveys and executives, new CEOs get little or no help from their boards when they are hired. Survey respondents (Bridgespan Group, 2014) portrayed nonprofit boards as disengaged or not equipped to support the new leader. Board members assume you know what you are doing. Some association board members have never hired anyone; others have not been in a hiring situation in years. Once the new leader is hired, boards typically step away out of fatigue and burnout from the search itself. However, you need time to get oriented, and you need their guidance. As part of your on-boarding, you will need to understand the priorities for your first six months on the job, and the board should help set your agenda.

Understanding and Agreement on Expectations

Key projects and the priorities of your work should be discussed with the executive committee and written into a document. The full board should be aware of this agreement and approve it. This document would be referred to at your 60- or 90-day review. Unfortunately, it is common to encounter boards that really didn't know why the CEO was hired. Seriously. They hired someone to do association work, but they didn't clarify the priorities. If this is what you walk into, it is up to you to clarify what they want you to do. Fail to get clarification of your first six months' goals could mean second-guessing, lots of unspoken expectations, and certainly a poor review because board members will all have a different opinion on what success looks like.

Don't have a document? Here are some suggestions for developing one. If you have a staff, you can find out what they consider to be priorities. Then discuss those ideas with the chairman, presuming agreement between the staff and chairman. If you can't get direction from the staff, tell the chairman that you both need to set the goals for success.

Get a feeling for where the organization is headed. Are there any urgent issues that need to be handled now? If not, what are the big revenue areas that need to be checked on? Is planning for the annual conference underway? Are sponsorships all secured and paid? If a legislative session or regulatory review is coming up, does preparation need to be done? When is the next audit? Just talking with the staff or chairman about the work over the next six months will produce a list of goals.

Review the status of the strategic plan. Is there work still to be completed? Is it a priority or has something else eclipsed it? Based on those discussions, you and the chairman can outline your priorities.

Developing a goals and priorities document also serves as a great segue to discussing your evaluation. As long as you are discussing priorities, ensure that the goals set are what you will be evaluated on for the first six months. When the priorities document is approved, you have your marching orders. If your evaluation was not discussed during your initial interview, talk about how and when your performance will be formally evaluated. Set the date and determine who will be doing the evaluation. If you have agreed on the priorities, your performance expectations and goals should be clear, providing concrete measurements for the board to assess your performance.

Don't assume board members like what you are doing and trust you if they don't address your performance and don't have an assessment planned for you. It is their responsibility to evaluate your performance, and if they haven't planned it, remind them. Ask for a review with the executive committee at 60 or 90 days, then a formal review after six months. If you don't have an evaluation form, ask your state association for a sample. The first six months will pass in a blur, but believe me, you need to get feedback from the executive committee or board—written feedback.

Building Relationships

Developing a good working relationship with the chairman is important, but good relationships with the entire board also need to be created and maintained. If you have a structure where a chair-elect is chosen and then moves automatically to the chair position after a year as chair-elect, you have a great opportunity to start building a working relationship early. You should talk with the chair-elect about his or her upcoming year four to six months before he or she becomes chairman. Plan a meeting with the chair-elect and create a list of items to review. Note that when you are new, you will need to jump in and have this conversation with the current chairman. Going over all these things really gives you time to get to know each other and understand how to best work together. Ask about the chair's goals and how they fit the strategic plan. You'll also want to have a discussion on the mission, bylaws, policies, and budget. Is the chair knowledgeable about the financial condition of the association? Does he or she understand the reserves and the largest revenue sources? Are there areas of concern?

Clarify how the chair and chair-elect want to interact with you. Get down to the details. How often does the chairman want to talk with you? Daily? Weekly? Certain time of the day? Does he/she prefer to talk on the phone, Skype, or just email back and forth?

In talking with the chair-elect, go over any obligations that come with being chairman: travel expectations, articles for the magazine, and speeches to give. Discuss whether the chair-elect is comfortable with being the spokesman for the organization and whether he/she may need speech coaching. Can that duty be delegated to the CEO or do bylaws prohibit the transfer? Look at the calendar together so the incoming chairman will know what is coming up during their year as chairman, especially board meetings and the annual conference. (Don't schedule next year's board meeting dates until you are sure the incoming chairman is available.) Review the board reimbursement policy (if there is one) and how hotel and travel arrangements are made for the chair and chair-elect. You will want to get into details about the board meetings as quickly as you can. Talk about committees, and if the incoming chair is to name members of the committees, what is the timeline for that?

Make note of any personal likes you encounter such as food and drink preferences, alcohol and non-alcohol, or special hobbies. If you are able to meet the officers' families, even better. Some organizations have a family-oriented culture, and spouses/partners/children attend many events. Others associations tend to stick to business, with little family involvement in association functions.

As the new CEO, ask how often the board should be updated. A state association board that had been through several CEOs in just a couple of years, asked their new CEO to send out a weekly report with updates on everything that had been done that week. They had been burned before, and they wanted to make sure that their new executive was working. They acknowledged that this could be perceived as overkill (and overwork), but they were hopeful that within a few months those reports could be tapered off once trust was established. They needed confirmation, and the CEO knew that if he were to be successful there, he needed to send those reports.

Discuss with the chair and chair-elect how to handle any disagreements with board members and what your role is. For example, if you have a board member micromanaging and asking a lot of miscellaneous questions at a board meeting or posting negative comments online, determine whose job it is to address the behavior. A best practice is for the chairman to handle any situations like this, member to member. It is good to discuss these things before the issue comes up. Review the bylaws about how a director can be removed from the board. If this topic is not covered, ask your attorney what laws pertain to governing your type of organization and what you should do if the bylaws are silent.

Part of the fun of working with the leaders of an organization is collectively setting the new leadership agenda. During your meetings, talk about what strategic accomplishments they are excited about and what they really want to get involved in. Discuss how the executive committee functions and if changes should be made in communications, reports, or other procedures. It's true that this litany of questions can seem overwhelming to a new CEO, but remember that information is king. Think of each answer as a bit of clarity. Slowly, you will emerge from the murkiness of being the new kid on the block, and you will be able to see clearly the entire picture of your new role.

Get a Feel for the Culture

The early months of a CEO's tenure can be difficult. You have to deal with institutional traditions, unspoken preferences, and the underlying concern of some people that you are going to wreck their association. It is important for you to understand the association and get a feel for its culture. Remember that visiting with board members in their offices or at conferences and events builds personal relationships that continue throughout your career as a CEO. Also shadowing members and experiencing what they do on a daily basis is very informative. Talk with past chairmen and board members about how the association functions, the processes, and the expectations, many of which were put in place by your predecessor. If that predecessor was much admired, you need to acknowledge that and be mindful and cautious about making changes without member support. Use that same cautious observation on almost everything during your first year with the association. Many traditional activities were established by volunteer leaders, and changing those without input and discussion could get you in hot water. The tightrope that you have to walk is knowing at what speed you need to act for various situations. This is important, but often difficult to measure. Again, ask questions and listen.

When working with a board, it is helpful to know what successful organizations do. According to the book, *7 Measures of Success,* published by ASAE: The Center for Association Leadership, great associations:

1. Understand their mission.
2. Are purpose-focused, not profit-focused, and do a few things really well.
3. Don't assume; are data-driven.
4. Have a strong culture.
5. Have leaders who seek to influence, not control.
6. Seek member involvement.
7. Have a "stop doing" list. (As new things are added, they must be accompanied by the removal of things from the current "doing" list.)
8. Change in a disciplined way and know what not to change.
9. Are not innovators but are great executors.
10. Are humble.

Board Meetings

How often your board meets should be spelled out in the bylaws. In between board meetings, the executive committee usually has the right to make decisions on behalf of the board and then those decisions are ratified at the next board meeting. Refer to the bylaws to ensure that these procedures are spelled out. If there is no mention of them in the bylaws, talk with the chair about how things get accomplished between meetings. In an ideal situation, the bylaws will guide you, but if they are lacking, put these procedures on the agenda when the bylaws are revised.

Nothing is as demoralizing to a board as inefficient meetings. Wasting their time is more destructive than you realize. Conversely, a dynamic and effective board meeting can energize the entire organization. Therefore, you should spend time preparing for each board meeting. The agenda provides for accountability and will serve as an outline in preparing the minutes for each board meeting. As you outline the work to be discussed, try to anticipate how much time will be needed for discussion. Provide enough time for each item.

You will develop the agenda with the chairman. It is very important that he or she has input and reviews the agenda before it is sent to the board. Always distribute the agenda and supporting documents in advance of a meeting. Usually one week ahead is acceptable, but your chairman and executive committee should be consulted about what they consider acceptable. If members are traveling, this ensures they get the information in plenty of time to read the materials.

Putting together a comprehensive board packet takes a lot of time (reports to complete, financials to complete, background material to research and compile). To have effective meetings, materials should be studied by the board members prior to the meeting. I think the majority of associations today send out electronic packets or have a Dropbox or Google account that board members can access. If that is the case, you will want to send your board a reminder that all the materials are available to be accessed and remind them of the date, time, and location of the meeting.

Talk to the chairman and determine how long the meeting should be and how long they historically have been. Each board situation is different, so there is no right or wrong amount of time. Average board meetings last three to four hours, but many associations have full-day meetings and some have two-day meetings. Keep in mind that you probably won't change anything for the first board meeting, especially if it has been set up and board members already may have made their flight reservations and allocated their time. But if you see that substantial changes would be beneficial, discuss the issues with the executive committee and plan to have the board review your recommendations.

Find out if there is a social aspect to the board's meeting. Is there usually a dinner the night before? Golf? Is lunch or breakfast included? The sooner you know these things and notify the board members about the schedule, the better planning they can do.

If the chairman is new, gauge whether he or she is comfortable running a meeting. Some volunteers have never chaired a meeting and may feel intimidated. Help your chair understand the flow of the day and all aspects of the agenda, anticipate things that might be contentious, and talk about the what-if's. Make sure you and the chair understand how motions are made and how to graciously but firmly cut off unnecessary talking.

Consider providing an annotated agenda for use by the chair alone. I often write up short notes about certain items and add them to my chair's personal agenda to give him/her hints and reminders. Review with the chairman the agenda format/outline that was used in the past, and if you have suggestions for improvement, discuss them. If there are options for organizing the agenda, consider grouping items into three sections:

1. **Action items.** This section would include items that the board needs to vote on and approve and could include minutes from the last meeting, the financial reports, annual budget, and audit. All reports to the board asking for approval should include who is making the recommendation, history or background information, analysis of issues summarized, and fiscal impact.

2. **Discussion items.** Discussion items may include strategic plan updates, future thinking suggestions, and legislative updates. For these reports, the situation is presented (what is it, what should it be, what we do) in a document. Give background on the situation and present discussion questions. (Is the problem clear? Do we need more information? What are action items?) Be strategic in discussion. Doing committee work or, worse, talking about mundane things like conference themes or locations for the board retreat should be avoided in board meetings.

3. **Information items.** This section includes reports of committee or staff work that has been completed. There is usually no discussion on this section of the board materials. All these committee and staff reports should be included in the board materials that are sent out prior to the meeting for the board to read before the meeting. They are for information only unless there is a recommendation and action needed.

Review and Oversight

I like to go over the contents of the board packet with the chairman a few days before the board meeting. He/she gets to see everything that will be in the board packet and ask me for clarifications. As the chair runs the meeting, he/she should be comfortable with the background and areas that need explanation and should also understand the intent of each report (which are action, discussion, or information items). A worst-case scenario occurs when an agenda item comes up and the chair looks surprised and has no information about it. Don't embarrass the chair like that.

One of the most important things to understand is that the chairman, not the CEO, runs the board meeting. The chair calls on key people who give reports or clarification. That said, it is helpful for you, the CEO, to sit next to the chairman so that you can write a note or mention something that he may need to be reminded of. I have heard executives say that their chairman was disengaged or asked the CEO to run the meeting instead. It is your job to help train the volunteer leader how to run the meeting, and if they are uncomfortable, encourage and support them. Do not let them delegate that responsibility to you. When their year is over, those board meetings will be a source of pride and growth for them.

Always plan for the unexpected to occur at board meetings. If a contentious item is being discussed and emotions are boiling over, have a plan to call a break. This gives the chairman a chance to re-group with the executive committee and/or talk with the people who may be arguing to calm them and hear their concerns.

Meeting Minutes

The purpose of minutes is to have an official record of the actions taken by the board. They are taken as a record for those who were there and those who did not attend. They are not intended to be an exact account of who said what. They should record the decisions made, not all the discussion. You don't need to include who made or seconded a motion. However, if a member wants to have a dissenting vote recorded, it should be noted.

Use the agenda to draft the minutes. Each agenda item should have a discussion or action explanation for it in the minutes. Minutes should include who attended, the location and time of meeting, what subjects were discussed, and the actions taken, including motions made. Include any presentations or reports, who made them and the fact that the board discussed the proposed action. Minutes should be concise and accurate so that anyone, whether or not they were present, can understand what decisions were made. Think of minutes as the historical record of the board.

Executive Sessions

The subject of executive sessions is confusing and unnerving to some people. In a worst-case scenario, a CEO may discover he is out of the loop when the board calls an executive session, asks him to leave the room, and when it reconvenes, tells him that he no longer has a job.

The confusion involves the very basic premise of holding an executive session. Executive sessions have their purpose, but the way some boards handle them, it's hard to decide if they're a best practice or a bad habit. Often there is a lack of clarity about what an executive session should be for. What is the purpose? Who should and should not be included? And should they be held regularly or only as needed? As part of the governance and policy-making structure, executive sessions should be addressed. Specifically, determine under what circumstances they could be held and who should participate in conversations about sensitive matters.

Asking the staff, including the CEO to leave a board meeting runs the risk of damaging trust between the board and staff. Certainly, there are situations when the board would like to talk candidly, without staff. But if this exclusion comes as a surprise, it can be taken as a lack of trust. Even worse is when the board does not tell you what was discussed or the outcome of the discussion.

For most instances, the CEO would stay in all executive session meetings. So, what kinds of discussions would need to excuse other staff or guests? Topics suitable for executive session include any type of litigation involving the association, perhaps crisis management, some contracts, and alleged improper activities. The CEO is usually asked to leave the room when the board wants to discuss the CEO's annual evaluation/compensation or succession planning, but these items should be on the agenda and not a surprise. As a general rule, executive sessions should not be held regularly, certainly not at every board meeting.

The time invested in getting to know the board, having solid policies to refer to, and taking the time to prepare everyone for board meetings is important. You will have lots of other things pulling you in a multitude of directions. Take the time to prepare a good agenda; have strong, well thought out supporting documents; study the financials and strategic discussions; and be prepared for questions. If you don't have the answers, promise to get the information and then share that as soon as possible. The more knowledge you have going into a board meeting, the more relaxed you will be. This is one of the few times that you are in front of the board, so you want to be at your best. Work extra hours to ensure that you are prepared. A confident CEO who provides good, timely information; keeps the board up to date; engages the board in dynamic discussions; anticipates questions and has the answers; and assists the chairman is what they were looking for when they hired you. Make the most of this opportunity.

CHAPTER EIGHT

Tackling Financial and Legal Issues

*Take the time to get a good grasp of the financials of the organization. You
can have the greatest programs in the world, but if the association is bleeding
money every year, you will not be around very long.*

– Frank Rudd, CAE
President & CEO
Florida Society of Association Executives

SSOCIATIONS HAVE THEIR OWN SET of rules when it comes to legal
and financial issues. They resemble the requirements for American
corporations and nonprofits, but they differ in substantive ways. There
are several excellent books pertaining to each subject, and you can learn more
by studying them, but this chapter will give you an overview of some of the
most frequently discussed areas. For more in-depth financial information I
recommend reading ASAE's *Financial Management Handbook for Associations
and Nonprofits, 2nd Edition.*

Association finance is one area where there are differences in the
actual presentation of the documents by each association, but the basic
understandings are similar. Finances are the backbone of the association.

Budget

Every association has an annual budget. Most associations have a finance or
budget committee, and you will work with them each year to create the next
year's budget. If you have professional staff, they are responsible for creating
their departments' budgets and then justifying them to the CEO before being
added into the full budget. Sometimes the creation of the budget falls to the
CEO, who then takes it to the board for approval (without a budget committee)
before the next fiscal year. The budget is a roadmap outlining financial revenue
and expense expectations; therefore, it is prepared for a 12-month fiscal year.
The budget outlines the timing of expected revenues and expenses spread
throughout the year. Budgets are prepared either on a cash basis or accrual
basis, the same way your actual financials are reported.

You will probably have an operating budget (showing details of all revenues and expenses) and a capital budget which shows capitalization and depreciation of fixed assets (assets that will last longer than one year and have a value greater than a certain amount established in your financial policy). The capital budget shows what fixed assets will be purchased or leased.

Whoever does the budget needs to be mindful of the priorities in the strategic plan and the mission. There are several budgeting models and you will need to review your current association model and determine whether it is giving the board a clear picture of income expected and the expenses associated with the programs and services including office overhead.

Each program or service will have its own detailed budget. When preparing the budget, it is a good idea to have notes that accompany the line items. For example, for the annual conference, you have a line item for registration fees income. Let's say it is $450,000. The notes can outline how you came up with that figure (X number of full member registrants at $, x number of nonmembers at $, pre-conference rates and onsite rates). Six months down the road, we often scratch our heads and wonder how we came up with some figure in the budget—the notes are invaluable to determining if we made a mistake or if we set an unattainable goal.

You will end up with an overall association budget with departmental program and service attachments that have detailed line item income and expenses. This budget should be monitored by all key department staff and the CEO throughout the year. They should follow all programs as they progress and be aware of any variances of revenue or expenses compared to budget.

All boards have the responsibility to review and understand the financial situation of the organization. While the CEO should be monitoring the financial situation at all times, monthly financials are a good guidepost to send to the board. Then at the board meeting, the board will review the most recent financial report. When emailing the in-between reports, I like to add a short note to the email with the highlights of the report that includes something like this:

Actual revenue and expenses to date; actual compared to budgeted in both. And any variance explanations if the variances from the budget are large or unexpected (for example, a cancelled event; low registration/attendance; expenses lower than originally budgeted).

There are two types of finances: accrual and cash. The accrual basis gives a better picture of the organization because it recognizes income when it's earned and expenses when they are incurred. A cash basis of reporting recognizes income when received and expenses when paid. (Example: $100 conference registration fee received on Jan 6, 2016, would be considered revenue on a cash basis in 2016. But the conference was held in November 2015. On an accrual basis, the $100 registration would be recognized as revenue in 2015.)

Some associations have a finance committee that meets regularly to review the finances. To me, the more board members looking at the finances the better. You should have nothing to hide, and if a project or program is not producing as expected, you want to give the board a heads-up and talk about ways to promote, incentivize, or come up with another plan.

Reserves

Although this topic was touched upon briefly in Chapter Two, reserves are an area of great interest. Ideally, every association has some money in a reserve account. Many have money that they invest for long-term growth.

Smaller associations may not invest in stocks, but they should have some money in reserves. If not, at a strategic planning session discuss how to build reserves and why you need money in reserves. A rule of thumb is to have six months' operating expenses in reserves so in case of an emergency, you would have a cushion to fall back on and keep the doors open. The board will determine what the goal might be for reserves, how the reserves can be used, and how to raise the funds.

Audit

A good rule of thumb is to have a financial audit done each year, or at least every other year. (Bylaws should specify this requirement.) This independent evaluation of financial information is performed by an independent certified public accounting firm. If you are searching for an auditor, look for someone who has experience with associations, not just nonprofits in general. An audit will review several internal controls, including the reliability of your financial reporting and compliance with laws and regulations. Reliability of financial reporting means looking at transactions to ensure that they are properly recorded, processed, and summarized and that assets are safeguarded against loss from unauthorized acquisition, use, or disposition. Compliance looks to see that transactions are done in accordance with laws, bylaws, regulations, and government policies.

You will need to prepare for the audit by gathering many pieces of information. The auditors will give you a list of things they need to review. This is known as an audit request list. Below is an example of items from such a list.

Audit Request List
- Detail general ledger
- Trial balance
- Balance sheet, statement of activities for combined and individual activities

- Bank reconciliations for each bank account
- Bank statements and investment statements
- Accounts receivable detail schedule
- Prepaid expenses detail schedule
- Furniture and equipment schedule
- Accounts payable listing
- Detail for other liability accounts
- Deferred membership dues and deferred revenue detail
- Quarterly payroll reports (941, 940, Workers Compensation)
- Forms w-3 and w-2
- Explanation of dues categories and dollar amounts for each, number of members paid
- Detail on education courses, such as number of attendees compared to last year, registration fees, and any expense information
- Detail on annual conference revenues and expenses, number of attendees, sponsors and exhibitors
- Board meetings minutes from past year
- Board of directors list
- Copies of any new grants, contracts, and leases
- Budget for fiscal year's ending
- Invoices for all fixed asset additions this year
- Any changes to bylaws and articles of incorporation
- Labor allocation schedule
- Functional schedule of expenses
- Checks to employees (non-payroll) with supporting documentation
- Checks and support for payments to credit cards

If you are a new CEO, and there has not been an audit in a while, you would benefit from an audit at the beginning of your tenure to ensure you are starting with a clean set of records and can identify any concerns or changes that need to be made.

Fraud

There has been a lot of publicity about associations (nonprofits in general) involved in fraud. Fraud can be committed by volunteers and/or staff. Three factors must be present for an ordinary person to decide to commit fraud: 1) incentive and pressure to commit fraud; 2) rationalization to support fraudulent actions; and 3) the opportunity to execute fraud without being caught.

The last factor is one that, with oversight, separation of duties, and policies and controls, can mitigate fraud. Whether it is a trusted employee or a volunteer, the possibility of fraud is an issue that you cannot ignore. While there is insurance coverage for employee theft, the bottom line is that you want to ensure you have enough safeguards in place to make it difficult for someone to commit fraud.

In any association, you want to ensure separation of duties so that one person is not handling all facets of money collection and recording. For example, one person can open the mail and record the checks in a check log, sending one copy to the CEO. Another person can enter checks into the accounting software, and another could deposit the money. The bank statements should never be opened by anyone other than the CEO, who can then check the statements against the copy of the check logs. In larger association staffs, the CFO will probably handle all bank statements.

Many associations have events where cash is paid onsite. Pay particular attention to the process and oversight of these transactions. Within the first few months of being hired by the pest control association, we had a fundraiser event. A lot of items were paid in cash, and I recall that first year, we had about $50,000 in cash at the end of the evening. The volunteers were all heading to the bar after the party, but I stopped three board members and advised them they had to help count the money and reconcile it to the sale of each item. All three of them assured me that my assistant and I could count it ourselves ("Of course, we trust you"!), but I was persistent and reminded them of their fiscal responsibilities.

It took us about two hours, but at the end, I had signed documents and printed calculator slips showing the cash, credit card income, who bought what items, and how they paid. The front desk made copies for everyone, and we put the money in the hotel safe. When the bank deposit was made, I sent each board member a copy, and when the financials were completed, I let them throw away their documentation. I had not thought through this fundraiser ahead of time, but in the moment, I had clarity of thought about oversight, and I was not about to be solely responsible for that money. You should always have multiple people overseeing any type of money collection and have a written process for how in-office and on-site transactions should be handled.

Sponsorships

Not every association sells sponsorship opportunities, but most do. This is income from vendors or suppliers who provide a product or service to your members, and in turn, they receive special recognition, promotion, access, and other benefits. Sponsorships have become sophisticated over the years, and many associations employ a business development or sponsorship specialist to maximize their possibilities. It's important to develop and maintain relationships with key sponsors as well as collaborate with them on what levels and kind sponsorships can be developed for them.

Sponsorship income can be substantial, and the association should have written and signed agreements with sponsors outlining what benefits they will receive in return for the investments they are making.

One large-staffed association executive found out the first week on the job that one of the association's subsidiary foundations had just announced a decision to "exclusively endorse" one of its largest vendors. What the foundation board didn't anticipate was the backlash that would ensue that week. All the other similar product vendors were upset that they had not been endorsed or even notified of the opportunity or process. As a direct result, they dropped their memberships, cancelled their sponsorships, and boycotted the tradeshow that was to take place in two weeks. These were the largest vendors in the tradeshow and, therefore, huge portions of the show floor were empty. The total amount of money lost to the association was over a million dollars in actual income that year. Strong oversight of the business development arena is critical, and fair treatment to similar/related entities should be a priority.

Political Action Committees

Many associations have created political action committees (PACs) to solicit funds and make candidate contributions for federal or state offices. There are specific guidelines and laws for setting up PACs, and close attention should be paid to state and federal filings, since enforcement fines can be high. Detailed guidelines for the administration of PAC funds should be developed and should include information about solicitations, contributions, expenditures, reporting, and how the funds should be established.

UBIT

Unrelated Business Income Tax (UBIT) pertains to money you receive that you should pay taxes on. The IRS will impose UBIT liability on certain activities of a nonprofit if those activities are found to be business activities unrelated to the organization's exempt purpose. This could include money from publications and ad sales.

Record Retention

For practical reasons, associations should keep records only for as long as is absolutely necessary. A policy should be in place that outlines what should be kept and for how long. Nevertheless, some things should never be destroyed. These include such things as board minutes, audit reports, financial statements, annual reports, articles of incorporation, bylaws, and pension plan documents. It is always wise to contact your attorney or accountant for record retention guidelines specific to your organization's needs and adhering to local, state, and federal laws.

Some sample retention items and the duration of their storage:

- Accounts receivable and payable (7 years)
- Articles of Incorporation (permanent)
- Audit reports, from independent audits (permanent)
- Bank deposit slips (7 years)
- Bank statements, reconciliations (8 years)
- Cancelled checks (generally 8 years)
- Cash disbursements journal (10 years)
- Cash receipts journal (10 years)
- Determination letter from the IRS, and correspondence relating to it (permanent)
- Employee expense reports (7 years)
- Employee payroll records such as w-2, w-4, annual earnings records (7 years)
- Financial Statements (permanent)
- General journal or ledger (permanent)
- Insurance policies (permanent)
- Invoices (7 years)
- Minutes of board meetings and annual meetings of members (permanent)
- Payroll journal (7 years)
- Payroll tax returns, including 941, 940 (7 years)
- Employment applications (3 years)
- Employee files (7 years after employment terminates)
- Pension plan (permanent)
- Real estate leases (10 years from termination)
- Tax returns (permanent)

Financial Policies

Too many associations get in trouble because the board of directors does not recognize why they need good policy and procedures. I recall one association that continued to lose money because the board did not insist on reviewing the financials. By the time they did insist on seeing the financials, all the reserves had been depleted. Although no fraud had been committed, they were asleep at the wheel and monies were spent because they had not established solid financial policies (especially for the use of reserves).

Another large state teachers association had always sent association logo items to their chapters to sell. T-shirts, coffee cups, and backpacks were all sent to local volunteers who were to sell them and send the money back to the state office. The problem was half of them never returned the money or any unsold items. The staff was frustrated because they didn't want to embarrass their volunteers by confronting them and didn't want to tell the board that money was being lost. They had no policies in place, no enforcement, no checklist of what was sent. They set themselves up for years for being poor stewards of the association's assets, and they lost thousands of dollars. It took the arrival of a new CEO to question what was going on and insist that policies be established and followed.

Financial integrity is built on solid financial policies. Policies are a subset of the organization's governing documents (bylaws, articles of incorporation). Policies guide volunteer leaders, especially the elected treasurer and the finance or budget committee. While every organization will have unique policies based on their situation and concerns, here are few common policies you should have and why you should adopt them:

- **Travel Reimbursement.** Establish guidelines for volunteer leadership and association staff regarding travel, food and beverage, registrations, advances, reservations, and reimbursements. It is important to be clear about what will or will not be reimbursed so that all volunteers understand the expectations beforehand.

- **Finance Committee.** A policy should spell out the function of the finance committee and what its role is. Clarifying who is responsible for oversight will avoid any confusion. For example, the policy should spell out that the committee develops the annual budget in conjunction with the CEO. It should also note if it is responsible for monitoring and making budget adjustments during the year. Also spell out if finance committee members monitor the performance of investments; and/or select and collaborate with a CPA/auditor.

- **Document Retention and Destruction.** To comply with laws affecting your association, adopt a recommended record retention and document destruction schedule, including checks, receipts, tax returns, and other documents,

- **Audits.** Having a financial audit is a best practice in association management because it ensures fiduciary responsibility. This policy will outline the need for the periodic audit, review, or compilation of the organization's finances. An audit committee should be appointed to work with the selected independent auditor and to present the final audit for approval by the board of directors.

- **IRS Form 990.** This is a mandatory filing, so this policy should clarify that before the submission of Form 990 to the IRS, the board will have the opportunity to review it.

- **Check-Signing Authority.** This policy should state who has the authority (officer or employee) to sign checks as well as define the number of signatures required. It should also address the processes for reimbursements, including the required submission of receipts in a timely manner. Similar authority would apply to the issuance and use of credit or debit cards. Don't forget to have a procedure for review of the CEO's credit card usage and reimbursements, typically by an executive committee member or finance chairman. Associations often require two signatures on all checks, especially those that are paid to the CEO, to ensure all checks are reviewed. This policy protects the CEO and the association from any accusations of misuse of funds.

- **Savings Reserves.** Many associations want to ensure that there are funds set aside for emergencies or future initiatives. This policy would state that the association will maintain a savings reserve equal to six months or more of annual operating expense (also referred to as overhead expenses) or 50 percent of net assets.

- **Investments.** If you have funds in excess of your savings reserve, the board may want to invest it. The board should adopt an investment schedule to address savings and reserves to best safeguard the funds. The investment policy should explain the types of investments that are allowed based on the association's risk tolerance. Some associations are comfortable with investing only in certificates of deposit, and some are fine with mutual funds and stocks. In addition, the investment performance should be reviewed periodically, and a meeting with the investment advisor should be held at least annually.

- **Independent Contractor Status.** There should be a policy that any person working as an independent contractor shall meet the criteria established by the IRS confirming independent versus employee status. Such a policy protects the association from possible lawsuits by contractors as well as challenges by the IRS.

- **Insurance.** Because the board is responsible for vigilance in avoiding risks and protecting assets, there should be a policy requiring the purchase of insurance coverages, including general liability, director and officers liability, fire, disaster, and event cancellation.

Even with the best policies in place, circumstances change and a policy may need to be re-evaluated. One situation that comes to mind was when an association was under financial duress. Because of the economy, revenues were not strong and there was concern that the association would have a deficit year. (That was not planned and budgeted.) However, the association had long had a policy that board members would be reimbursed for all travel expenses to board and committee meetings, which added up to a very large expense each year. The CEO talked to the chairman about asking the board members to refrain from submitting any travel reimbursement requests for the rest of year. This suggestion was not received well. The chairman believed that because the policy had been in place for years and that the board members gave of their valuable time, they needed to be reimbursed. Bottom line, if you reimburse volunteers for expenses, and you don't have a wealth of reserves, the situation could become sticky.

This scenario could provide a good "what if" discussion during budget meetings. Best case scenario would be to have a policy that addresses withholding member expense reimbursement if association's finances are not meeting budgeted projections.

A few reminders about finances that are good rules to live by include: Live within the budget and notify leadership regarding any significant variances; have checks and balances to avoid any perception of improprieties; provide scheduled, regular financial statements to leadership; ensure the association has adequate reserves; ensure access to necessary outside financial advice.

Legal Issues

As a new CEO, you need to be aware of legal areas that could get you in a lot of trouble. I'm not an attorney, but I can tell you that the nature of associations is unique, and understanding their legal, antitrust, and taxation issues are specialty law areas. It is wise to contract the services of an attorney who specializes in association representation. A great resource book is *Association Law Handbook, 5th Edition,* by Jerald Jacobs, which you can purchase from the American Society of Association Executives.

Contracts

It is common for a new CEO to be surprised by the many contracts associated with association management. From hotel contracts to speaker or entertainer contracts, from contracts with vendors (including decorators, transportation, food and beverage, printing, accountants, lawyers) to sponsor agreements, from office purchases or leases (computers, software, equipment)to employee, research, and consultant contracts—you can be overwhelmed by contracts. Because the use of contracts is so widespread, it is wise to have an attorney on retainer to review any contracts you are signing. Keep in mind that only select people should have the authority to enter into a contract for the association. The CEO should have the authority to sign all contracts. Other staff should not sign any legal agreements, and in most cases volunteers should not sign contracts on behalf of the association.

One area where executives can get the association in trouble is hotel and meeting contracts. These are usually complicated and are written for the protection of the hotel/meeting facility. The standard forms usually include several areas where you could be setting the association up for huge financial loss (for example, room attrition). Watch out for clauses like the cancellation term dates and percentages owed if you cancel or do not meet the room pick up or food and beverage minimums. Spending the money to have an attorney explain the various parts of a hotel contract will be well worth it. This guidance will give you the support you need to negotiate changes in such contracts.

Three weeks after 9/11, a state counseling group was scheduled to have its annual convention. The income from the tradeshow and registration was substantial to the association. But their members were counselors, and many had volunteered to go to New York and Pennsylvania to assist grieving survivors. Only a few days before the event, the association staff realized that half of their hotel rooms would be empty because members cancelled their reservations. Of course, this also meant that attendance revenues would be substantially lower than budgeted. The hotel contract had severe penalties for room attrition (rooms contracted but not used) as well as the loss of food and beverage income. The association had not been prepared for this unforeseen tragedy (How could it have been?), but its staff had signed the hotel contract without any corrections, strikethroughs, or negotiations. This contractual obligation never should have been accepted unless the association was sure it could cancel or negotiate with the hotel to reschedule.

In this situation, the association did not want to reschedule the meeting, which might have allowed them to possibly negotiate with the hotel to accept the rebooking instead of a cancellation. They chose to pay the penalty for not picking up the minimum number of rooms they had contracted and the reduction in food and beverage sales—a cost of more $75,000. For many associations, an unexpected expense like this could be disastrous.

Terminating Employees
The CEO has the responsibility for hiring and firing; therefore, you must be aware of potential liability when terminating an employee. If you are unfamiliar with employment laws, be sure to get advice from your attorney or the state employment commission before acting.

The employment "at will" principal still governs most employment situations; however, many states now recognize employees' rights and may penalize employers for wrongful discharge. When a problem arises, you should act quickly to identify it, discuss it, and resolve it. Delaying action can disrupt the office environment and may disrupt the association. Meet with the employee and spell out your expectations for performance and a timeframe in which those expectations must be met. The timeframe should not be long, perhaps a couple of weeks or a month depending on the circumstances. Check back in to discuss performance. Your expectations should be in writing and use terms like "behavior modification." If corrections are not being made, continue to follow up with increased and stronger warnings about the seriousness of the problem and the consequences if it is not corrected. Put all conversations, counseling, actions, and expectations as well as warnings and discipline in writing. The employee should receive copies as well. You need to have this documentation in case of legal action. The employee should be told very simply that they will be let go unless behavior and work improvement is noted.

Antitrust

When members get together at meetings, discussions cover a broad range of issues dealing with their industry or profession. Participants in association meetings at all levels must be made aware that discussions of certain subjects could raise concerns of antitrust and should be avoided. Understanding when the discussions veer into the realm of private regulation will help you and your members stay out of trouble. Some areas of concern include denying membership services to nonmembers, pricing of activities, membership restriction and termination, product certification, professional restrictions and credentialing, and group buying and selling. You cannot have discussions at association meetings that might indicate raising, lowering, or stabilizing prices or fees; regulating production levels or affecting the availability of products and services; encouraging boycotts; setting current or future prices, cash discounts, or credit terms; or refusing to deal with a company because of its pricing practices, to name a few examples. For many groups, constant monitoring by legal counsel is needed, and you should seek expert advice when questions are raised about what subjects and discussions are or are not appropriate. When in doubt, always refer to your attorney for guidance.

As the CEO, you need to pay close attention to all legal risks and try to avoid them, including exposure from social media use. Think about speaker materials that you might post on the website. Do you have permission or is that a copyright violation? What is your legal position regarding members who complain or post false claims on your Twitter or Facebook pages? One association actually had a young board chairman who posted angry messages about the association on the association listserver. Communication policies might be the best proactive action you can take.

If your association does not have an attorney, you must ask your peers for recommendations and find an attorney who is well versed in association law. Awareness, training, and policies are best practices for staying out of trouble, but particularly as a new CEO, you cannot run an association well without strong legal counsel. Consultations with your association's attorney will help guide your interactions with staff, members, and vendors. Having an attorney on call may not make your work trouble-free, but it can certainly help you avoid obvious pitfalls until you are comfortable making experienced decisions.

CHAPTER NINE

Taking the CEO Journey

Teamwork is key. Ask questions and take advice from seasoned members and colleagues.

– Diana Everett, PhD, CAE
  Executive Director
  Texas Association for Health, Physical Education, Recreation and Dance

A s a new CEO, it is easy to be overwhelmed with what you have to learn, evaluate, and implement. You are on a journey, and along the way you will experience many wonderful things, learn aspects of professions that you never thought you needed to know about, gain wonderful skills, meet many inspiring people, and make lifelong friends and wonderful memories. You will also be frustrated, tired, angry, and let down. With the right support systems in place (people and policies), however, you will feel great satisfaction at the end of each day.

The association profession is unique and can be a wonderful career. You may stay with an association your whole career, or you may have the opportunity to work with a variety of fascinating organizations. Whatever path you go down, be assured that there are resources to help you.

At first, you will need mentors to help guide you and friends who will grow right alongside you. Your initial mentors may be the board leaders. They will help you learn about their association and profession. But within the first month, you will need to have a group of other association CEOs that you can call on for advice about working with members and staff or running an association. This could include your colleagues in other states that work for the same association, but it should also include people down the street or across town who work for another association. If you don't know any other association CEOs, contact your local or state society of association executives and ask for a referral, connection, or introduction. Attend meetings that are offered, especially if there are CEO-only sessions or events. Check out the state and national annual conventions; a multiday educational experience will give you time to meet and build relationships with others. Look for online communities

(ASAE and your state professional society), where you can post questions and peers will offer assistance. If you are invited to events by affiliate members (hoteliers, convention and visitors bureaus) try to attend because you will make valuable business connections for your organization as well as other association executives.

Many new CEOs plunge right into their day-to day-responsibilities and don't look for outside education and help for several years. That's unfortunate. But you are reading this book, and that means you have made a commitment to learning and to improving yourself and the association you work for. Part of being a successful CEO is continuous learning.

If you are new to the association profession, one credential that you should seriously consider getting is the Certified Association Executive designation (CAE). This is the highest credential in the association profession, and it is taken seriously. Offered by the American Society of Association Executives, almost every state society and many local affiliates offer assistance in studying for the exam. The exam is offered twice a year (May and December). But you need to understand the eligibility requirements and time commitment. You need three years as an executive director or five years as an association staff person as well as 100 hours of continuing education before you can apply. A lot of reading is required, and attending a study course is helpful. Not only will you meet other executives in the study groups but you will receive good guidance on how to study, and areas of concentration. Plan to start on getting your continuing education hours and consider taking the course and exam as soon as you are eligible. You will learn about principles of association management as well as legal and financial issues. Your board should support you in obtaining this designation, both by paying for the exam, books and study course and in allowing you the time to attend the study sessions. Upper-level staff can also benefit from having a CAE designation, so discuss this educational certification with them.

The day-to-day work flow will vary for every new CEO. If you are the CEO of a smaller staffed association, your day-to day-job will be getting the work done—from the financials, to meeting planning, website, communications, meetings, and phone calls. It may be hard to focus on overall governance issues when you are managing the office each day. But I encourage you to spend time on discussing the need for review and setting up any new processes or policies. It may take you a year or more, but be diligent about getting policies written and training the board members.

More advice comes from Kerry Stackpole, FASAE, CAE, a longtime association executive and president of Neoterica Partners. He notes the importance of being attentive to the board's behavior by noting that newly appointed CEOs need to be extremely sensitive to the past—specifically the systems, processes, and expectations—built by their predecessors. He posted a blog about gaining trust at www.wired4leadership.com. Stackpole's recommendation is to communicate, communicate. But, he stresses, do it tactfully and diplomatically, meeting with all key executives and informal leaders in the organization. The tone and tenor of your initial contacts go a long way in carrying your message and setting the stage for your leadership and the organization.

That's good advice for a CEO navigating his or her honeymoon period, which ends...well, when? When does the on-boarding or transitional period end for a CEO, to the point where earning the board's respect isn't the primary concern?

Stackpole's answer: Slower than you might like, and perhaps never. The transitional period is done when the board begins to endorse and actively support the ideas of the new CEO. Notice he didn't say "accept." Accepting is far too passive and lacks the essential elements of enthusiasm and commitment to assure success for the new CEO. The truth is that the board's endorsement of your ideas is rarely unanimous.

When it comes to getting to the point of active support, Stackpole makes a distinction between the speeds at which the new CEO needs to operate—fast when it comes to understanding the board intimately and slow when it comes to implementing new ideas. Doing the opposite may force you to play defense. If a CEO hasn't worked early in their tenure to quickly build understanding of board members, strengthen personal relationships, and mold a general consensus for the future, the only "safe" route for the CEO is to make small changes at the margins and move slowly toward their implementation.

That doesn't mean you need to be timid going in, but your actions need to be meshed with passion for the organization you're leading. That's what the board members will be looking for when they first get to know you, Stackpole says. And of course, they'll want it for years to come as well. I agree with Stackpole when he says, in many ways, the CEO is earning the board's respect every day.

Words of Wisdom

Over the years, I have compiled a folder of "words of wisdom" from association executives around the country. The list that I tend to refer to the most is from Bill Taylor (deceased), former president and CEO of the American Society of Association Executives. I share these tips with you to encourage you, to let you know that you are in good company, and to assure you that you are not alone.

- Know that you are not alone. There is a large association executive community ready to help you.

- Meet fellow CEOs whom you can call on for guidance.

- Two areas where CEOs get in trouble: not watching the financials and board governance.

- Hire the best staff you can. Give them authority, but hold them accountable.

- Don't be reluctant to use consultants to solve problems when you don't have the expertise.

- Don't ever forget that the association belongs to the members, not you.

- Use volunteers effectively and respect their time.

- Create a "kitchen cabinet" of member advisors. It might take a while to determine who they should be.

- Prioritize your responsibilities.

- Accept external responsibilities with high visibility to build the stature and recognition of your association; public relations is part of your job.

- Never forget that wherever you are or whatever you do, as CEO, you personify the association. Virtually everything you do will be a credit or discredit to it.

- Take public speaking assignments seriously. Avoid being unprepared.

- Emphasize time management in your own schedule and your staff's.

- Be friendly. Be humble.

- Be entrepreneurial, take chances; the association will progress faster and you'll have more fun.

- Develop follow-up techniques for your own responsibilities and volunteer leaders; lack of follow-up destroys organizational effectiveness.

- If you must compromise, do it with grace.

- Be charismatic; attempt to make every contact a pleasant experience for the person you are speaking with.

- Remember you are setting the example—with your attitude, your work habits, and expense account.

- Study other associations. Adapt the best ideas.

- Communicate.

- Your integrity is your most important asset.

- Don't expect to know everything early on. It takes at least six months (maybe a year) for things to come together.

- Don't be afraid to say, "I don't know."

- Remember that the process can be as important to the members as the decision reached.

- Don't expect leadership to adapt to your way of doing business; you will have to adapt to their way.

- Realize that the members want it all, they want it now, and they want it for almost nothing.

- Never say what you wouldn't put in writing. Never put anything in an email that you don't want to see in print or have to defend in court.

- Do more listening than talking.

- Recognize that you cannot make all people happy.

- Create your own rewards, as you may not get credit for good work/deeds.

- Beware of hidden agendas with members and staff.

The association profession is one of sharing, so learn from these parting thoughts from association CEO's who have been in your shoes:

Don't come in guns blazing to right all the wrongs you see in your first week. Remember decisions are made with the best information available at the time. So quickly take time to learn the history of the association, meet past as well as present leaders, and review past board meeting minutes so you are better prepared to navigate the road ahead.
 – Leslie Murphy, FASAE, CAE
 President
 Raybourn Group International

Strategically plan for yourself. Enhance your knowledge and keep your skills current. Don't allow a hectic schedule serving others and moving your organization ahead erode time and emphasis from a healthy lifestyle and a plan that keeps you at your best.
 – Joan Tezak, CMP, CAE
 Executive Director
 Colorado Society of Association Executives

Ask good questions. Good questions lead to goals and metrics that propel you forward.

Also, listen. There are two sides to every story and as the new CEO, listen. This works for board, staff and member issues.

    – Mary Lange, CAE
    President
    Independent Bankers of Texas Foundation

Don't do it all yourself, especially if you are the only staff member. Recruit volunteers and delegate, delegate, delegate.

    – Kristen Joyner
    Executive Director
    Southwest Transit Association

The number-one job of a CEO, whether in a small or large organization, is to be a consummate politician. Mastering that skill will serve you well throughout your career.

    – Gary Godsey
    Executive Director
    Association of Texas Professional Educators

To all new CEO's, I emphasize the importance of a mutually agreed upon employment contract. With this initial contract, the foundation of trust and partnership is established.

    – Bill Keese, CAE
    Executive Director
    Association of Progressive Rental Organizations

Lean on and trust the strengths that got you to the position; you will develop the rest in good time.

    – JJ Colburn, CAE
    Executive Director
    Texas Association for the Gifted and Talented

*Always ask your board **what** your association should do; never ask them **how** to do it. Cultivating a micromanaging board will eat up the valuable time you need to develop and launch innovative member benefits. Ask lots of questions to a variety of association stakeholders. In addition to gaining practical information, you'll find thought leaders who can help identify crucial opportunities for your association.*

    – Mark Allen, CAE
    Executive Director and CEO
    International Order of the Golden Rule

Look at current staff through the lens of strength and resiliency before determining inadequacies. You will need every bit of their collective wisdom to get off to a positive start.
- Tracy Todd, Ph.D. LMFT
  Executive Director
  American Association for Marriage and Family Therapy

You have to be nimble—lively, brisk, swift, alert, and awake!
- Jim Coles, CAE
  Executive Director
  Texas College of Emergency Physicians

Your team will work hardest to achieve a vision they helped create.

Communication is key. At the top you see the bigger picture. Keep your team energized and on point through effective communications. And remember that effective communication is a dialogue, not a monologue.

At times you will bog down. Take time to reset yourself to maintain clarity.
- Mike Grubb, CAE
  President and CEO
  Southern Gas Association

My first goal was to schedule meetings with all the previous board chairs— around 20 people. I wanted to gain their trust, their organizational knowledge, and their assurance that I would respect the core values of the association that they helped instill while using them as a sounding board for new ideas. I found the meetings both educational and instrumental in forming those important relationships with association leaders.
- Ward Tisdale
  President
  Real Estate Council of Austin

Past presidents or chairmen are treasures. They have valuable experience and can be enormously helpful to CEOs. Besides, they know where the bodies are buried.
- Doug McMurry, CAE
  Executive Vice President
  AGC San Antonio Chapter

The key to low anxiety and being able to sleep well at night as an association CEO is always remember, "it's their party." Know when to step in front and lead and know when to get behind and facilitate.

   – Tom Morrison
   CEO
   MTI Management

Establish a regular communications plan with your president/board chair or executive committee, and use it.

   – Larry C. Smith
   Executive Director
   International Practice Management Association

Take care of yourself. You can't be a good leader if you are stressed out, tired, or demoralized. Work out, eat smart, get enough sleep, and take some vacation. This will both allow you to give work 100% and to show your staff you believe in work/life balance.

   – Margaret Bonds Podlich
   President
   BoatUS

As a new CEO, your new eyes will see an endless number of possibilities. Don't act on too many too soon. You'll make yourself crazy trying to take advantage of every opportunity, and won't have the context to prioritize.

   – Lori A. Ropa, CAE
   Executive Director
   The Arc—Jefferson, Clear Creek & Gilpin Counties

You will never know everything, and don't pretend that you do. Engage and encourage open discussion with your members, board, and staff. Effective ideas come from all levels of an organization. You never know when looking at an issue from a different perspective will bring clarity. It is always worth taking the time to listen.

   – Tami R. Lutzi
   Executive Director
   KBA/NBA Schools of Banking, Inc.

Association management is being prepared, foreseeing upcoming obstacles and staying relevant with your membership. Failure to outwork the competition and predict the future is costly. Association management has changed so rapidly during the past five years. Execs, like fortune tellers, look into crystal balls for tomorrow's challenges. Being resilient sometimes means being patient and waiting for the right opportunities.
  – Fredrick Pausch
  Executive Director
  County Engineers Association of Ohio

The old adage, "Always put a member between you and a problem," rings true over and over again. Until you are the CEO, this may seem a nebulous and aspirational idea. It's not. Being able to tactfully and diplomatically deploy your volunteer leaders in service of the organization is a critical part of your success as a leader.
  – Wendy W. Kavanagh, CAE
  President
  Georgia Society of Association Executives

As someone who has been an association professional for more than 30 years, I have found association management to be a fascinating and ever-changing job. I hope that this book gave you guidance, wisdom, and reassurance. A new CEO needs all three.

APPENDICES

Assessing Where the Association Stands

As a new CEO, you will need to assess just where the association stands especially in finances, staffing, programming, technology, membership, and communications. This book gave you an overview of all the nuances of association management and your role as the new CEO.

However, to fully understand what the structure of the association looks like (and give you an idea of where improvement can occur under your leadership) an internal assessment should be done.

This internal assessment will give you a good handle on the systems in place and what documents and processes exist. Just knowing that all the governing documents are easily obtainable (and everyone knows where they are) creates peace of mind. As the new CEO, doing an assessment will give you—and the board—an overview of what is in place (a benchmark for when you started) and what still needs to be done. It is a strategic baseline and will serve as a guide for you and your work.

One option is that you can hire consultants to do a full internal assessment for you. Having an external company handle the assessment could be an excellent choice, as it will provide a third-party perspective in its report. If the association has never had a financial audit, it is highly recommended that you have a financial audit conducted as well. Again, this is a great report to give the board (and you) an overview of the condition of the association.

Should you desire to do an assessment yourself, this information will serve as an overview of some of the areas that you should inventory. It will help you identify your documents and processes, and the resulting report will be valuable for you, your staff, and the board. You can easily make this a checklist, with notations next to each item saying where it is stored, when it was last updated, or if it is missing.

And finally, I have added a list of reminders of things to do the first few weeks on the job. While this was intended for small staff executives, several of the reminders apply to all staff sizes. It is not comprehensive but will help you get started.

Internal Assessment Checklist

Governance Documents
- Articles of Incorporation
- Current bylaws
- Compiled board policies (preferably in a policy manual)
- Certificate of sales tax exemption for 501(c)(3) organizations
- Strategic plan
- Board commitment form
- Sample board agenda
- Board minutes
- Board evaluations
- Procedure manuals (finance, personnel)

Public Record Documents
- Letter of determination
- IRS Form 990
- IRS Form 1024 and/or Form 1023 if the association is classified 501(c)(3)

Legal and Internal Documents
- Insurance policies
  - Director and officers liability
  - General liability
  - Event or meeting cancellation insurance
- Board policies
  - Antitrust
  - Conflict of interest
  - Apparent authority
- Contracts
  - Software
  - Copyright
  - Equipment
  - Recent hotel or meeting contracts
  - Speaker agreements
  - Affinity/non-dues income programs
  - Sponsorships

Finance
- Annual budget
- Financial reports
- Recent audit

- Record retention policy
- Financial procedures manual
- 401(k) or retirement plan documents
- Recent compensation and benefits survey of associations
- Sales tax certificate, which may be required if you sell books, clothing, or other products

Organizational Documents

- Lease contract or mortgage documentation
- Organizational chart
- Succession plan for CEO or key staff
- Personnel handbook or manual
- Personnel files (including job descriptions, evaluations, Forms w-2 and w-4)
- List of bank accounts
- Document with key contacts information (auditor, attorney, IT consultant, accountant, banking contacts, retirement plan administrator, health insurance company), and computer passwords

Getting Started:
Things to Do in the First Few Weeks

ESPECIALLY IF YOU ARE A one-person shop or have only one or two employees, a lot of the information gathering will be instigated and done by you. Just knowing what to ask can be an issue for a first time CEO, so here are some guidelines to follow for the first few weeks:

Staff, Consultants, Projects, and Contracts

- If possible, meet with the outgoing CEO or interim executive director to get updates on pending work, upcoming deadlines, and the status of projects.
- Complete the necessary paperwork for employment, including i-9, w-4, and direct deposit.
- Determine who the association employs as outside contractors, such as accountants, lobbyists, lawyers, or educators, and arrange meetings with them.
- Review current contracts and future meeting space contracts for annual conference and/or tradeshow, technology, equipment, and affinity programs.
- Review staff files, job descriptions, and evaluations.
- Review the employee manual.
- Review the association's annual calendar. If you don't have one, start one. It should include committee and board meetings, annual conference and other educational programs produced by the association, national association convention, holidays and other office closings, board nomination deadlines, and publications/communications deadlines.
- Meet with the entire staff individually to review their job descriptions and responsibilities.
- Develop a teambuilding event for staff.

- Review travel policies and reimbursement policies for staff and members as well as credit card usage, travel reimbursement forms, and rules for submission.

Office and Technology

- Determine who has keys to the office or building security cards and the check-out process.
- Locate maintenance, cleaning, and landscape company contacts.
- Obtain contact information about who handles your IT needs. Find out about computer security, changing passwords, and remote access. Find out about back-up of files, cloud storage, or how files are stored. Locate the website domain registrations and any other agreements that have annual renewals, such as contracts with survey companies or e-commerce agreements.
- Locate or create a document listing all the association's fiscal and physical assets.
- Determine what equipment is owned and what is leased.
- Find out what association management system (AMS) is being used and determine whether it is current and working well. Be careful about making any quick changes in this area until you understand the full scope of needs/resources/cost.
- Review dues policies, membership categories, billing processes, dues proration, and application processes.
- Find out who maintains the website content.

Finance

- Review association financials, budget, and past audits with your accountant.
- Review payroll and taxes, policies on accounts payables and receivables, cash flow situation, sales tax and tax deposits, property taxes, most recent tax returns, and filing requirements.
- Review investment accounts and money market and CD accounts. Review all bank accounts and learn about the check writing process. Identify who is authorized to sign checks and what the amount limits are. Change signature cards.
- Determine all the association's revenue sources, such as dues, nondues income, product sales, educational programs, tradeshow, publications, and royalty income.

- Determine if the association uses a lockbox for dues processing.
- Determine if the association has a safe deposit box and a P.O. box for mail.
- Find out guidelines and timeline for fundraiser events, if applicable.
- Review similar information for all related organizations (foundation, PAC, for-profit subsidiaries).

Board

- Meet with chairman and executive committee to agree on goals for first six months.
- Review the strategic plan and progress.
- Meet with treasurer to review budget, accounts, and recent financials.
- Find out who appoints standing committee chairs, how volunteers are selected to serve on committees, travel reimbursement policies for board members , and complimentary registration practices,
- Review board orientation, including when it is done, who does it, and who attends.
- Discuss the plans or the need for a board retreat.

Legal and Legislative

- If you have attorneys on retainer, meet with them to discuss their responsibilities and fees; determine if there are any pending legal issues.
- If you have lobbyists, meet with them to review their responsibilities and fees and get updates about regulatory and legislative issues. Also discuss the political action committee (PAC) and required filings.
- If the association doesn't have a lobbyist, determine who is responsible for carrying out the advocacy work/lobbying. Who determines what the definition of success is with advocacy initiatives? Have the required reports been filed? If you are to serve as the lobbyist, find out about lobbyist registration.

Resources

7 Measures of Success: What Remarkable Associations Do That Others Don't. Washington, DC: ASAE: The Center for Association Leadership, 2006, 2012.

The Power of Associations. Washington, DC: ASAE: The Center for Association Leadership, January 2015.

Associations Matter. Washington, DC: ASAE: The Center for Association Leadership, January 2012.

Operating Ratio Report. Washington, DC: ASAE: The Center for Association Leadership, 2012.

Agard, Kathryn. *Leadership in Nonprofit Organizations: A Reference Handbook.* Thousand Oaks, CA: SAGE Publications, 2011

Coerver, Harrison, and Mary Byers. *Race for Relevance: 5 Radical Changes for Associations.* Washington, DC: ASAE: The Center for Association Leadership, 2011.

Coerver, Harrison, and Mary Byers. *Road to Relevance: 5 Strategies for Competitive Associations.* Washington, DC: ASAE: The Center for Association Leadership, 2013.

Cox, John B., and Susan S. Radwan (eds.). *ASAE Handbook of Professional Practices in Association Management, 3rd Ed.* Hoboken, NJ: Wiley, 2015.

Dalton, James G., and Monica Dignam. *The Decision to Join: How Individuals Determine Value and Why They Choose to Belong.* Washington, DC: ASAE: The Center for Association Leadership, 2007.

Frankel, Jean and Gabriel Eckert. *From Insight to Action: Six New Ways to Think, Lead, and Achieve.* Washington, DC: ASAE: The Center for Association Leadership, 2012.

Gazley, Beth and Katha Kissman. *Transformational Governance: How Boards Achieve Extraordinary Change.* San Francisco: Jossey-Bass, 2015.

Gazley, Beth and Ashley Bowers. *What Makes High-Performing Boards: Effective Governance Practices in Member-Serving Organizations.* Washington, DC: ASAE: The Center for Association Leadership, 2013.

Jacobs, Jerald A. *Association Law Handbook, 5th Ed.* Washington, DC: ASAE: The Center for Association Leadership, 2012.

Jacobs, Sheri and Carylann Assante (eds.). *Membership Essentials: Recruitment, Retention, Roles, Responsibilities, and Resources.* Washington, DC: ASAE: The Center for Association Leadership, 2008.

Lang, Andrew S., and Wayne Berson. *How to Read Nonprofit Financial Statements, 2nd Ed.* Washington, DC: ASAE: The Center for Association Leadership, 2010.

Renz, David O. and associates. *The Jossey-Bass Handbook of Nonprofit Leadership and Management, 3rd Ed.* San Francisco: Jossey-Bass, 2010.

Sladek, Sarah. *Knowing Y: Engage the Next Generation Now.* Washington, DC: ASAE: The Center for Association Leadership, 2015.

Stevens, Craig, et. al. *Financial Management Handbook for Associations and Nonprofits, 2nd Ed.* Washington, DC: ASAE: The Center for Association Leadership, 2011.

Tecker, Glenn H., Paul. D. Meyer, Bud Crouch, and Leigh Wintz. *The Will to Govern Well: Knowledge, Trust, and Nimbleness, 2nd Ed.* Washington, DC: ASAE: The Center for Association Leadership, 2010.

New Board Orientation Outline

Introductions—Icebreaker

Mission
Vision

Strategic Initiatives

Who's on the Board
Resource/background. Include photos

Governance
- Duties
- Purposes—sign commitment form
- Conflict of interest
- Antitrust
- Legal considerations and policies

Finance
- Financials
- Budget

Staff and responsibilities and programs
- Education
- Membership
- Communications
- Administration

Committees/Task Forces

Calendar of Events/Board meetings

Resources
(review of orientation book)
- Bylaws
- Policies
- Past minutes

CEO update
- Hot topics; immediate projects
- New programs
- Travel reimbursement policy

Board of Directors Commitment Form

I understand and accept the duties and responsibilities of the board of directors of XYZ and will serve in the capacity to the fullest extent of my abilities.

I understand this is a working board and not an honorary position. As such, I will attend regular board meetings, educational seminars, annual convention, and other programs presented by the association.

I understand that notice must be given to the president for absence from a board meeting prior to the meeting date. I further understand that absence from two consecutive board meetings without notice will be automatically considered as resignation from the board of directors.

I understand that business of XYZ may be of a confidential nature and will share only appropriate information outside board meetings.

I understand that policies and business decisions must be made in the best interest of the membership of XYZ, and I will fully support all decisions made by the board of directors.

I understand that should I ever find myself under obligation to any other group or organization that is in conflict with XYZ, I shall disclose the conflict to the board and refrain from voting on issues related to the conflict. (See Conflict of Interest Policy.)

Knowing that XYZ is member driven, I will be an active promoter of membership acquisition.

In the event I cannot uphold these responsibilities, I will resign and relinquish my post.

Signature ＿＿＿＿＿＿＿＿＿＿＿＿＿＿＿　　　Date ＿＿＿＿＿＿＿＿

Board Agenda

AGENDA

XYZ Association

XYZ's mission: _____

Date: _____   Location: _____

Time: _____   City, State: _____

Welcome and call to order by Chairman. *Determine that a quorum is present.*

(9:00 am) Introduction of guests/new board members/announcements.

I. Association Business/Action Items

A. Approval of minutes from xxx BOD meeting	*action item*	*responsible person's name*
B. XYZ Financials	*action item*	*responsible person's name*
C. Topic Example: Board Nomination Slate	*action item*	*responsible person's name*
D. Topic Example: Audit Report		*responsible person's name*

II. Strategic Discussion

A. Strategic Plan 2015–2017 (status update, and remaining work)

• XYZ _____	*responsible person's name*
• XYZ _____	*responsible person's name*
• XYZ _____	*responsible person's name*

III. Leadership Reports

IV. Informational Reports
A. Education
B. Membership
C. Nondues Income

    D. Legislative

    E. Communications

V. Discussion/New Business

VI. Adjourn
Next meeting date

Board of Directors Meeting Evaluation Form

Date: _____

1. Pre-meeting communications	YES	NO
Was all information distributed prior to this meeting regarding location/time/agenda/etc. helpful and communicated in a timely manner?		
Were the agendas well-planned and clear?		

Comments:

Please rate the following questions 1–5, with 1 being poor and 5 being excellent.

2. Meeting	1–5
Did the meeting facility meet your needs?	
Did the board chair run the meeting effectively?	
Did you feel free to contribute, or voice concerns?	
Was staff participation appropriate?	

Comments:

3. Content	1–5
How helpful was the content presented to you as a board member?	

Comments:

4. Please rate the meeting format/content/discussion for the following sessions.	1–5
Association business—financial, minutes	
Strategic plan review and discussion	
Committee and task force updates	
Leadership updates	
Informational department reports	

Comments:

5. About you	1–5
How would you rate *your* preparation for this meeting?	
How would you rate *your* participation in this meeting?	

Comments:

6. How can future Board of Directors meetings be improved?

7. Any other comments or suggestions?

Request for Proposal—Audit

Background

XYZ Association (XYZ) is requesting a three-year proposal from several CPA firms that have extensive experience in providing audit and tax reporting services for associations.

XYZ is an association classified as a 501(c)(6) tax-exempt organization by the IRS and is headquartered in (City/State). The organization employs approximately X employees.

The most recent audit was performed by X, who will have an opportunity to re-bid on the engagement. In the event they are not selected, X will cooperate with the new auditor by providing access to their working papers and discussing any significant issues relative to our audit and tax work.

The Association concentrates on standards, codes and related technical endeavors, government affairs, economics and market development for approximately X member organizations engaged in X. Members are invoiced xx times a year.

The Association manages an education foundation with minimal activity and net assets. An audit of this entity is also requested to be part of your bid.

Association policies are determined by a board of directors composed of CEOs of member companies. The XYZ CEO/Executive Director is the senior staff executive. Key operating elements include the executive committee, the finance committee, and the chairman of the board and the president. The association's approximate share of budgeted operating expenses are as follows: Operations (x%), Educational Programs Services (x%), Communications (x%), Government Affairs (x%).

Financial Status

XYZ revenues for fiscal year xxxx were approximately $x million, and expenses amounted to approximately $x million. Association revenues were comprised of the following: Dues (x%), Meetings and Exposition (x%), Publications (x%), and investment income primarily accounted for the remaining x percent.

XYZ writes an average of x checks per month. The association's semimonthly payroll is processed by an outside vendor and the payroll is paid primarily through direct deposit. The association earns unrelated business income in the form of advertising and, therefore, files an annual Form 990-T.

Computer Equipment and Accounting Software
In 2015, XYZ successfully transitioned its member and accounting databases to (name of AMS).

Retirement Plans
XYZ sponsors a defined benefit plan and cooperative 401k savings plan. We are not requesting as part of this RFP audit or tax work connected with these plans other than those procedures necessary for disclosure in XYZ's audit report and tax returns.

Timing
XYZ uses a calendar year which ends December 31. We anticipate that we would be prepared for the audit to begin fieldwork in early May xxxx and would expect the delivery of financial statements and management letter by June 30, xxxx. Tax returns are expected to be delivered at least five days prior to their due date for review by management with no more than one extension requested.

Sample CEO Evaluation

After reading the summary of accomplishments, please indicate how X met goals and expectations in each of the following areas of responsibility using the scale below.

Instructions: Please circle or highlight the performance rating for each area of responsibility. Descriptions of the ratings are provided as a guide. Comments should support given ratings. Please use additional sheets if necessary.

5	4	3	2	1
Exemplary Performer	Exceeds Expectations	Meets Expectations	Marginal Performance	Unsatisfactory Performance
Exemplifies leadership and predictably produces exceptional outcomes	Mastery of role and contributions beyond role; consistently exceeds performance objectives	Handles issues and responsibilities within role and delivers on standard expectations; consistently meets performance objectives	Performance is consistently below expectations in many areas of responsibility. Must address clear development needs to meet performance expectations	Continuously fails to achieve basic requirements of role with no signs of improvement

Section 1—CEO Responsibilities

Management and Leadership

1. Responsible for overall day-to-day management of the association, establishes the necessary criteria to review and evaluate the performance of the total organization and its major functional activities.

2. Responsible for decisions related to employee hiring, training, compensation, and performance evaluation.

3. Works with the general counsel/board and responds adequately to legal issues and related matters.

5	4	3	2	1

Budget and Finance

1. Directs the preparation of an annual budget for board approval and provides regular and timely financial reports to the board.

2. Ensures the maintenance of accurate financial records, the use of best practices related to financial management and controls, an annual audit by an external firm, and adequate responses to any issues raised in the Management Letter.

3. Negotiates all contracts in accordance with the wishes of the board of directors or as appropriate.

5	4	3	2	1

Board Process and Relationships

1. Develops and recommends to the board of directors long and short range objective, plans pertaining to the goals of the association and emerging strategic issues.

2. Clearly communicates the strategic plan and established metrics for monitoring progress toward strategic goals and utilizes the strategic plan to establish the budget and plan of work for the year.

3. In conjunction with the chair, plans and coordinates board of directors and executive committee meetings, including the development of agendas and appropriate level of reports and background materials.

4. Creates an environment for healthy relationships, constructive dialogue and knowledge-based decision making while bringing new ideas to the table and contributing to the board discussions and deliberations.

5	4	3	2	1

Member Relations and Benefits

1. Improves and increases the services the association provides to its members, ensuring programs and services that are relevant to the needs of a cross-section of association professionals at various stages of career and skill level.

2. Ensures that staff responds to member inquiries quickly, thoroughly, and in a professional manner.

3. Communicates policies and positions effectively both orally and in writing.

4. Conducts appropriate member and market research, ensures that programming and service are adjusted accordingly, and introduces new ideas in programming and services and leverages the use of technology where appropriate.

5	4	3	2	1

Public Relations and Representation

1. Initiates, develops, and contributes to advancing the association alliances and maintains and broadens the network of partners and potential partners in industry, associations, institutes, foundations, government agencies, etc.

2. Directs the association's promotion, publicity, and public relations activities, serves as the XXX spokesperson, and is well regarded by key external audiences.

3. Oversees the management of the association's legislative activities and serves as the organizational liaison to the xxxxxx.

4. Maintains effective relationships with key customer groups including exhibitors, advertisers, sponsors, etc.

5. Encourages members and staff to take leadership roles in related organizations and in other ways that benefit the association and the profession.

5	4	3	2	1

Section 2—Professional Traits and Behavior

Commitment to Quality

Displays enthusiasm for job; demonstrates dedication to the mission of the association; makes objective and effective decisions; seeks ways to improve the quality of work processes and environment; acts in the best interest of the association; monitors/updates applicable department sections of the association's operations policies.

5	4	3	2	1

Communication
Communicates appropriately and understandably verbally; listens effectively to others; writes and documents clearly and effectively when required; shares appropriate information with colleagues and leaders as needed.

5	4	3	2	1

Conflict Resolution
Is open to suggestions for growth and improvement; addresses potential problems proactively through appropriate channels; seeks effective alternative solutions (or compromises when necessary); gives constructive feedback to co-workers; takes responsibility for own actions.

5	4	3	2	1

Initiative
Takes responsibility to seek innovative and creative ways to do the job and solve problems; undertakes new projects outside routine job activities; follows up on projects and tasks; anticipates obstacles to the success of tasks and projects; exhibits appropriate independent thinking and action.

5	4	3	2	1

Teamwork
Seeks and considers different viewpoints; demonstrates regard and respect for the uniqueness of others; maintains confidentiality; works effectively with others; recognizes and respects the role of each individual; cooperates to achieve association goals; seeks assistance as needed and shares/delegates tasks appropriately.

5	4	3	2	1

Section 3—Specific Strategic Goals

1. Goal 1

5	4	3	2	1

2. Goal 2

5	4	3	2	1

3. Goal 3

5	4	3	2	1

Section 4—Comments

1. Please identify any examples that you believe are particularly noteworthy. Explain how they illustrate your evaluation above.

2. Please identify any achievements you believe should be recognized.

3. Please note any areas in which performance should be improved.

4. Please identify the most important goals you would set for the CEO for the coming year.

Submitted by _____   Date _____

CEO Employment Agreement

(Review by attorney is recommended)

This agreement is made as of (date), between the XYZ Association and Name (the executive employee).

In consideration of the mutual agreements make herein, and for other good and valuable consideration, the parties agree as follows:

1. Employment and Term: XYZ engages the services of Employee as its President/Executive Director.

Employee agrees to perform services for XYZ for a term beginning (date) and for a period of three years, ending (date).

After that three-year period, this agreement will automatically renew each year on (date) for additional one-year periods unless the Association or the Executive, according to the provisions in Section 5 or 6, cancels the agreement. The first day of the initial employment term, and the first day of any successive employment term renewed automatically shall be referred to as the "effective date of this agreement." Notwithstanding the foregoing, the Employee's employment term is subject to termination under Section 5 and Section 6 below.

2. Duties: For the term of this agreement, the Employee shall be employed by the Association in the capacity of President/CEO, subject to Section 6, and shall provide such services and have such responsibilities and duties as are normally associated with such capacity. In addition to any other duties that are set forth in the Associations bylaws and the job description and may be assigned by the Executive Committee from time to time, the Employee shall be responsible for a) implementing the policies of the Association, b) serving as advisor and assistant to the Chairman of the Board, c) acting with full authority for the management of the association offices, d) hiring and terminating all association personnel, and e) reporting directly to the Chairman of the Association. The Employee shall devote full time to the business of the Association and the performance of duties hereunder, shall discharge such duties in a diligent and proper manner, and shall endeavor to advance the best interests of the Association at all times.

3. Compensation: The salary portion of the Employee's total compensation shall be paid at such time and in such installments pursuant to the Association's general salary payment plan, subject to any adjustments as directed by the Board, and agreed to by the Employee. The salary of the Employee is $x per year during the first year of this agreement.

In addition to the Employee salary, a bonus payment ("bonus") may be paid to the Employee. Whether to award the bonus payment, and the amount of the payment, will be made at the sole discretion of the Executive Committee. Sole discretion means that the Executive Committee decides whether a bonus should be paid and, if so, in what amount under criteria set by the Executive Committee.

No later than (date), and each year thereafter, during the term of this agreement, the Executive Committee shall a) establish basic goals for the next fiscal year ending at the next date, b) determine, as part of the annual performance review of the Employee, the extent to which previous goals were met, and c) based upon that determination, determine the compensation to be paid to the Employee during the next succeeding twelve-month period. If the committee does not establish a salary for the Employee for the next succeeding twelve-month period, the Employee's salary shall be equal to the salary for the immediately preceding twelve-month period. In no event, will the Employee's salary for any subsequent year of this Agreement be reduced below the level of the previous year.

4. Employee Benefits/Expenses: As further compensation for employment services to the Association, the Employee shall receive the following benefits and expenses:

a. The Employee shall be entitled to participate in such retirement plan, group life insurance, hospitalization, disability and other group employee benefits as are presently or may hereafter be provided to other employees of the Association on a general basis, which benefits may be in varying amounts relative to the compensation otherwise paid to such employees.

b. The Employee shall be entitled to xx days of Personal Time Off (PTO) on a fiscal year basis. A maximum of one-half of any unused annual PTO may be banked for future use up to a maximum of xx days.

c. The Employee shall be entitled to reimbursement of reasonable business expenses, upon submission of appropriate receipts, including membership dues in _____ State Society of Association Executives, and ASAE, and work-related travel expenses.

5. Disability and Incapacity of Employee: This Section 5 shall govern any disability of the employee. As used in this Agreement, the terms "disability" and "incapacity" are used interchangeably and are both intended to be interpreted as "disability" as that term is defined in xxx group policy. If at the time there is no such policy in effect or it does not contain such a definition, then the last definition included in the most recent group term policy shall apply.

a. Continuation of salary: In the event that the Employee shall be prevented from fully performing his/her duties hereunder by reason of disability or incapacity, the Employee shall continue to receive full salary and full benefits under Sections 3 and 4 for a period of up to six months. If, after a period of six months, the employee is still prevented from fully performing his/her duties by reason of disability or incapacity, the Employee will be provided benefits as appropriate through the Association's disability insurance program and/or workers compensation insurance and her salary will be discontinued. Any salary or benefits required to be paid to the Employee pursuant to this Section 5a shall continue to be paid during the period of the disability or incapacity even though the employment term shall have expired prior to the expiration of six months. The Employee shall continue to be entitled to receive full benefits under Section 4a above until the Employee's employment terminates under Section 5 b or Section 6.

b. Termination of employment by reason of disability: During the employment term hereunder, if after the date of the Employee's disability determination the Employee has been unable to fully perform his/her duties for a consecutive twelve-month period, or if at any time after the date of the Employee's disability determination but prior to the end of the consecutive months from the date of such disability determination, the Association, acting through its Executive Committee, may notify the Employee of its intent to terminate the Employee's employment hereunder; provided, however, the effective date for any such termination shall be the later of thirty days after the date of such termination notice, or the end of the consecutive twelve-month period after the date of the Employees disability determination.

6. Termination of Employment:

a. Employee's employment term hereunder shall terminate upon the earliest to occur of any one of the following events:

  • The expiration of the employment term, including any automatic extension thereof, provided, however, that the Executive Committee must give the

Employee at least six months prior written notice that the Employee's employment term will terminate.

- The death of the Employee.
- Any termination by the Association under Section 6 (b).
- The Executive may cancel this Agreement by giving the Association a minimum of six months advance notice in writing, with any longer notice subject to the approval of the Executive Committee; the notice may extend beyond the then-current annual term of this Agreement and the Agreement will automatically be extended through that notice period only. The Executive will receive full compensation during that notice period; at its sole discretion, the Association will determine whether to require that the Executive perform the Executive's duties for the association during that notice period.

b. Notwithstanding Section 6 (a) above, the Employee's employment term hereunder shall terminate upon written notice of such termination and within the timeframe specified for the for the following events:

- Employment shall terminate immediately in the event of documented acts of dishonesty, fraud, or gross negligence that is, directly or indirectly, detrimental to the best interests of the Association.
- Employment shall terminate immediately upon the admittance by the Employee, or a judgment of guilt by a court of law, of a felony under state law or a Class A misdemeanor or a felony under United States law.
- Employment shall terminate three months from the date of written notice due to the Employee's continuing inattention to, or neglect of, the duties to be performed by the employee under this agreement, provided that termination under this clause shall not occur unless
  - The employee shall have been put on specific written notice of what constitutes the continuing inattention or neglect and it is not corrected, and
  - The employee is given a minimum of three months to accomplish such correction; or
  - Employment shall terminate three months from the date of written notice due to a disclosure of any confidential information by the employee in violation of this agreement, or any other material breach of employee's covenants or any of the other terms and provisions of this agreement.

c. The Employee's employment term hereunder may also terminate upon the election of either the Association or the Employee, upon a minimum of twelve months written notice to the other or any shorter period of time that the society and the employee may mutually determine, provided that should the society terminate the employment terms under this clause, the employee shall

- Cease immediately to hold the position of Executive Director/CEO and
- Perform such duties during the twelve-month period as the Association shall direct and as are reasonably related to assuring a successful transition in such office, and provided further that should the Employee terminate employment under this clause, the Employee shall continue to perform duties hereunder until the termination date.

The Executive Committee shall have full authority to take any and all actions on behalf of the Association under this section 6.

7. Effect of Termination: If the Employee's employment is terminated pursuant to Section 6 (a) or 6 (b) but not Sections 6 (c) above, then except as specifically provided in Section 5 or Section 8, this agreement shall be of no further force or effect, and the Employee shall have no obligation or duty to further serve the association in any capacity, not shall the association be under any obligation or duty to employ the Employee or make any of the payments provided in Section 3 or 4, except that the Employee shall be entitle to receive any accrued but unpaid compensation as of the date of termination, pursuant to and subject to any limitations contained in the provisions of the Associations policies.

8. Intellectual Property, Confidentiality, Noncompete: The Executive recognizes and agrees that all copyrights, trademarks, or other intellectual property rights to created works arising in any way from the Executive's employment by the Association are the sole and exclusive property of the Association and agrees to not assert any such rights against the Association or any third party. Upon cancellation of this agreement by either party for any reason, the Executive will relinquish to the Association all documents, books, manuals, lists, records, publications, or other writings, keys, credit card, computer stored data, software and hardware, equipment, or other articles that came into the Executive's possession in connection with the Executive's employment by the Association and to maintain no copies without the written approval of the Executive Committee. The Executive will maintain in confidence during the Executive's employment any information about the Association or its members which is confidential information or which might reasonably be expected by the Executive to be confidential.

9. Indemnification: The Association shall indemnify the Employee in the event that the Employee is a party or is threatened to be made a party to any threatened, pending, or completed action, suit, claim, or proceeding by reason of the fact that the Employee is or was an Employee of the Association, or was otherwise serving at the request of the Association, against expenses, including attorney's fees, actually and reasonable incurred by the employee in connections with the defense or settlement of such action or suit if the Employee acted in good faith and in a manner reasonably believed to be in or not opposed to the best interest of the Association, except to no indemnification shall be made in respect of any claim, issue, or matter as to which the Employee shall have been adjudged to be liable for gross negligence, recklessness, or intentional misconduct in the performance of the Employee's duty to the Association.

10. Applicable Law and Force of Agreement: This agreement shall be governed by and construed in accordance with the laws of the State of xxx and this agreement constitutes the entire agreement concerning the employees employments and supersedes all other agreements.

11. Dispute Resolution: Should there be disagreement of any portion of this agreement, then the parties shall enter into mediation previous to any filing of a law suit in the state of xxx. Mediation shall be in (city) and shall be in accordance with applicable rules of dispute resolution in (state).

In witness whereof, the parties have executed this Agreement in multiple counterparts as of the date first set forth above.

Date _____   Date _____

By _____   By _____
Employee   Board Chairman

ABOUT THE AUTHOR

 Beth Brooks, CAE, is the president and CEO of the Texas Society of Association Executives (TSAE). She has worked in the nonprofit arena her entire career—spanning more than three decades—and has led TSAE since 2002.

Prior to joining TSAE, she worked 10 years for the Texas Dental Association and 10 years with the Texas Pest Control Association. A member of ASAE and the Texas Society of Association Executives for more than 30 years, Beth is a Certified Association Executive (CAE) and is a frequent writer, speaker, facilitator, and consultant for association professionals and their boards. She understands the relationship between elected leaders and the volunteers who agreed to serve with them. But more importantly, she understands the role of paid executives and the staffs who serve them.

As a mother of one, she has been a volunteer for almost every school and sports-related committee, from athletics to academics, to even campus landscaping for the past 14 years.

She spends her free time traveling with her family, gardening, reading, curling (yes, even some in Texas do that), and swimming. She and her husband David have a son, Matthew, who is a junior in college.

Throughout her association professional career, she has survived 24 bosses—that is, one executive director at Texas Dental, and 23 volunteer chairmen (who each have their own ideas of how an association should be run...) at Texas Pest Control Association and TSAE combined.

She wrote this book to give others an idea of how to survive the challenges many CEOs never saw coming.